The Magic of Mediocrity
How business buffoonery bewitches us all

Robert Overton

Waderone Publishing

Published in the UK by Waderone Publishing, 2013

The right of Duncan Robertson (pseudonym Robert Overton) to be identified as the Author of this work has been asserted in accordance with the Copyrights, Design and Patents Act 1988.

© 2013 Duncan Robertson (pseudonym Robert Overton)

All rights reserved. No part of this publication may be reproduced in any form or by any means – now known or hereafter invented, graphic, electronic, or mechanical, including photocopying, recording, taping or information storage and retrievals systems – without the prior permission in writing of the publishers.

This book is reproduced using paper that is made from wood grown in managed, sustainable forests. It is natural, renewable and recyclable. The logging and manufacturing process conforms to the environmental regulations of the country of origin.

British Library Cataloguing in Publication Data. A Catalogue record for this book is available from the British Library.

ISBN 978-0-9576918-0-3

The names and identifying characteristics of the individuals featured throughout the book have been changed to protect their privacy. Any resemblance to actual persons, living or dead, is purely coincidental.

Illustrations by Mike Mosedale

Printed and bound in the UK by Ace Graphics, London

To order copies of the book, write to Waderone Publishing, 103 Brownlow Road, London N11 2BN, email waderone@brownlow103.freeserve.co.uk

Contents

Introduction		1
I	Twenty-first century icon: The Strategic Executive	3
II	Welcome to his world - a day in the life of a strategic executive	14
III	All that glitters ain't gold	29
IV	Away with the fairies - the self-delusional world of Personnel	42
V	Office-gate: the great office farce cover-up	60
VI	Dumbing down	70
VII	We don't need no education: the 3Rs in modern business	85
VIII	Wake-up call - the life and times of PowerPoint	99
IX	The court of King Caractacus	111
X	The root of all evil	125
XI	Essential office politics	139
XII	At large	152
XIII	Gas emissions - strategic executives and the environment	163
XIV	Turning the tables	177
XV	Top 10 ridiculous things about office life	191
XVI	Boys and their toys	201

Acknowledgements

I would like to thank all the strategic executives whose buffoonery has provided me with the inspiration for this book. For the sake of my career (and theirs) I dare not mention them here. I hope, however, that if they do recognise themselves, then they'll appreciate that it's much better to have a legacy of laughter than one of professional pretentiousness.

INTRODUCTION

"The general tendency of things throughout the World is to render mediocrity the ascendant power among mankind." Thus wrote John Stuart Mill and nowhere is this more evident than in the modern office. Boring PowerPoint presentations, grand promises not kept, lame jokes met with loud guffawing and, above all, reams of memos, manuals and e-mails devoid of interest, fact and linguistic coherence but not of hyperbole, arrogance and boasting. Welcome to the "Business World" (tantalisingly close to being an anagram of "Bullshit Words"), the place where mediocrity knows no modesty.

By contrast, how refreshing it would be to read some corporate literature which was either remotely interesting or showed at least a modicum of self-awareness. An annual report, business plan or marketing brochure which didn't view its subject company as being God's gift to the global economy but instead something average, below-par, in decline or middle ranking. Well, it's not going to happen, and so, in the absence of such candour, this book will endeavour to bring some perspective to life at work. It doesn't take itself seriously enough to pretend to be a "Self-Help Guide on How to Succeed in the Modern Workplace", but at least it may serve as a useful aide-memoire to see the funny side of it.

So why write a book about life in the office? Two main reasons. Firstly because mediocrity masquerading as excellence is often very funny, albeit almost entirely unintentionally. I speak from personal experience. I started working on this book when I had been in the "real World" for 23 years, 13 of them "at board level" (or should that read "bored"?) as a finance director. I am an insider, not a disillusioned drop-out writing a sour grapes sob story of a milieu which I can't find a place in. The depressing thing is that I'll need to work another 23 years before I can execute my exit strategy (retirement). Like a marathon runner hitting "the wall", I've come a long way but I have just as far to go.

Secondly, to ever-so-slightly redress the lack of written material on an activity many of us spend more time on than any other: sitting in the office. How strange that in this age of multi-media, digital gadgets, there are so few images or photographs of us in the one single place we are most often to be found: at our "workstation". How odd also that, whereas we will happily pass on to our friends any propaganda we fall victim to over the weekend or whilst on holiday, e.g. that we saw "Europe's biggest firework display" or "the castle which inspired Walt Disney", we are not so keen to pass on our own employer's rhetoric and brag about how we work for a company which, "passionately believes in delighting its customers by providing a seamless, turnkey, information solution"? Could it be that we want to somehow block it out? That we are in some sense ashamed.

Well, fear not: this book will make you proud of it. Not in the way that the typical business books do - by churning out rhetoric which makes you feel like everyone else takes work seriously and really believes in doing their best for their company. But one which hopefully puts a smile on your face when you realise that you are a bit-part player in the greatest comedy of all-time: the Great Office Farce.

I

TWENTY-FIRST CENTURY ICON: THE STRATEGIC EXECUTIVE

Today's Strategic Executive

Where better to start in illustrating the absurdities of the business world than bearing witness to the life and tools of the cornerstone of all this bullshit, the modern twenty-first century Strategic Executive. He is the Alistair Campbell of the business world, all style and no substance, except that Alistair Campbell's sole advantage (there's only one of him) is not shared by the Strategic Executive, of whom there are regrettably thousands.

So how do you spot a Strategic Executive? To summarise, he (they're overwhelmingly male) is the quintessential prat. Chambers 21st Century dictionary defines a prat as, "an ineffectual fool". Doesn't really convey the full horror of this phenomenon, so what follows is probably the most concerted attempt yet to capture the essence of that elusive term, the prat.

The career of the Strategic Executive

Fundamental to understanding the modern Strategic Executive is seeing where he's come from, how he got here. Unfortunately the primary documentary source for this information is the great fictional work known in the corporate world as CVs.

How can CVs be summarised? Well, a country's Gross Domestic Product (GDP), the statistic which officially measures economic growth and so determines whether or not a country is in recession, is calculated by adding up all the incomes of that country's households and businesses. However, they'd get a much more encouraging result if they added up all the stats which people write about themselves on their CVs. Businesses would be achieving exponential year on year growth, accompanied by soaring rises in profits and eye-popping increases in market share. There'd be a veritable tsunami of projects generating sustained multi-million pound savings over several years, with new flagship customers being won every day. Unemployment figures would be zero since nobody would ever get sacked or made redundant although there would be a suspiciously high number of people seeking fresh challenges with an unbroken track record of success. It's amazing that, with a country stuffed full of people with superb attention to detail skills and a real bottom-line focus, we've somehow collectively contrived to rattle up a debt of £32 trillion.

As for the CV of the Strategic Executive, it has much in common with the safety routine performed by air hostesses on an aircraft. Just as the 'plane is taxiing along to take off, the air hostesses assemble in the aisle with their various props. What should happen next is that the captain should announce, "in the event of an emergency, you will all die," whereupon the air hostesses would throw themselves screaming to the floor, enacting a sudden violent death whilst the TV screens show videos of people being decapitated, burnt alive or eaten by sharks. Brief and accurate.

What actually happens is much longer and completely fictitious: the pre-recorded announcement implies that adopting the brace position will withstand a 1,000 mph crash from a height of four miles whilst the air hostesses and a nice reassuring video playing soothing music showing how we'll all have ample time to put on each other's emergency oxygen masks, blow up our life jackets and politely remove our shoes before descending the evacuation slide. We'll even be provided with a nice

HEALTH AND SAFETY EXECUTIVE LAUNCHES
NEW IN-FLIGHT PROCEDURES

Before annihilation please ensure that all mobile devices are in flight safety mode.

whistle, if we fancy striking up a tune to keep spirits up.

Similarly misleading is the Strategic Executive's CV. It should do nothing more than shriek out in big red letters, "this guy will screw your business and piss everybody off in the process." But it doesn't. Instead it refers to a proactive business leader who has spearheaded high-profile projects with long-term value-add in order to drive accountability throughout the organisation and its supply chain, achieving year-on-year improvement in all key performance indicators across the business." Yeah, yeah – and where is he to be found now? Job Centre Plus.

So what lies beneath all this? Broadly speaking Strategic Executives got where they are today by one of two routes – birthright or sheer hard bullshit. The birthright brigade are the sort of people who have fewer than eight great-grandparents. In fact interbreeding is so rife in their circles that they don't really have a family tree, so much as a family trunk.

Whatever their family background, at school the Strategic Executive was the kid who would give the impression of being clever by always putting up his hand to answer the teacher's easy warm-up question and then remaining conspicuously quiet, whilst nodding knowledgeably, for the rest of the lesson. He would never complete his homework on time but would have a charming way of apologising for this.

He left school to get a "pass" diploma in Business studies, the academic qualification internationally recognised for denoting three years of intensive drunkenness. His CV got a massive and unexpected boost 15 years later when John Major's Sour Grapes Education Act reforms managed to undermine all the academic qualifications the then Prime Minister had failed to achieve. Mickey Mouse certificates were suddenly elevated into something sounding rather grand. And all of a sudden the Strategic Executive's alma mater, Poxy Town Poly, became the University of Western Europe and his old school, Sinktown Comp, was transformed into the Centre of Academic Excellence for Entrepreneurial Studies.

At "uni" (as he calls it, in an attempt to appear cool) he was one of those people who would spend his time at the Freshers' Fair signing up to 36 mutually incompatible societies including all three major political parties (and the Liberal Democrats) plus a few less desirable ones reflecting his more distasteful views. As a forerunner to one of his professional specialities, he subsequently never went to any of the meetings.

The actual job path of the Strategic Executive is shrouded in mystery (or repeated redundancies) since it is at the post-education stage that the CV degenerates into a combination of sheer fantasy and meaningless twaddle. The only thing that is sure is that the "freelance consultancy" periods are euphemisms for being unemployed or the odd spell in prison for credit card fraud.

At some stage in his career, he is likely to have done a Mish-mash of Bugger All, or MBA as it has come to be known as. This must be just about the only qualification where you pay the examiners and as a consequence, if you don't quite answer the questions correctly, they write to you or have a quiet word and you get to re-do it. Pity Chris Tarrant doesn't adopt this approach on "Who wants to be a millionaire?"

Somehow the Strategic Executive manages to find a wife – but not by proposing on bended knee. Instead he would have faxed through in four different and overlapping instalments a rambling "Heads of Terms for a Strategic Alliance building upon our complementary skill sets to gain real-time synergy across a broad spectrum of activities." Mr and Mrs Strategic Executive go on to have 1.8 equally obnoxious and uncombed children.

The final incongruity in the typical Strategic Executive's CV is his choice of referees. Having delivered all these multi-million-pound savings and brought in so many blue-chip clients for so many senior CEOs, how strange that he should choose as referees his brother-in-law and his former college lecturer, whom he hasn't seen for over 20 years.

How to spot a Strategic Executive

You don't need to be familiar with a Strategic Executive's CV to instantly spot them in the workplace.

Firstly there are one or two tell-tale sartorial signs. The fashion-sense of the Strategic Executive is truly lamentable. This has been a major driving force behind the changes in office dress code in recent decades. Basically over time Strategic Executives have had fewer and fewer items of clothing to worry about – compared to their 1960s counterparts, there are no waistcoats, cufflinks, braces and hats to wear and now even ties are dying out. In fact if you extrapolate this trend, by the middle of the present century Strategic Executives will be turning up to work completely naked. At least they won't be inflicting those horrible shoes with tassles on us any longer.

Having said that, Strategic Executives were – together with building site labourers - early pioneers of the hipster low-hanging belt, although in the case of the Strategic Executives, this was more as a consequence of the downward pressure being exerted by their girth rather than by any Dolce Gabana instincts or insight.

But the most definitive emblem of the Strategic Executive's attire is the food-stained tie, which like the number of rings on a tree trunk, gives away the age of its wearer. Ties cannot be washed and the Strategic Executive is too lazy and forgetful to take them to the dry cleaners. They therefore accumulate years of stains from being dipped in gravy, splashed by croutons falling in soup or by wine being thrown at them by various people their wearers have offended and insulted in the pub down the years. And there might be the odd bit of residual vomit, occasioned by Christmas parties.

In terms of personality, the Strategic Executive has a wide-range of defining characteristics. Here are just a few key traits to look out for.

The Strategic Executive has redefined conversation ethics, not just with his callous disregard for language and grammar, but with his partner-in-crime, the BlackBerry. In the olden days (the early 1990s) if you were talking to somebody and another unidentified person at some distance suddenly shouted your name, you would have ignored them, if indeed you even heard them. Not any more. It is now socially acceptable for the Strategic Executive to take a call whatever his situation thus leaving the other person to decide whether to listen in, walk out or pretend

BOYS: DO THEY EVER GROW UP?

they've suddenly and coincidentally remembered something to do. Actually the best response is to drop your trousers and start crapping in the corner: when the Strategic Executive looks suitably startled, just say, "Sorry but I thought we were both behaving as if the other person wasn't here."

The Strategic Executive goes on holiday to "7-star" hotels in Dubai, makes the candidates on "The Apprentice" seem modest and with hindsight, foresaw the 2008 banking crisis. If he'd been around during World War II, he would see himself as a Winston Churchill figure whereas the war leader who more readily comes to mind is Captain Mainwaring. He gets annoyed when given a name badge (because he thinks he needs no introduction) and considers himself above basic bodily functions – for instance, he never admits to sleeping, just taking the occasional "power nap".

The Strategy thing

The Strategic Executive has a variety of nob-a-job titles and has got where he is today because in the modern business world, strategy is king, or rather the word "strategy" is king. Any old crap can be transformed into something superficially awe-inspiring by association with the word "strategic". Don't work with a tinpot client, have a strategic account; don't have a half-baked, implausible idea, formulate a strategic vision and don't recruit a clapped out, middle-aged teletubby with a track record of total ineffectiveness, hire a Strategic Executive. Oh and the next time, you're caught surfing dodgy websites, call it Strategic grooming.

The ascendance of "strategic thinking" over actually doing anything is astonishing and unique to the business world. In war, for example, who would get the more plaudits? The top-brass general who sets out a fancy looking battleplan (probably on PowerPoint) and then, like Italy in World War II, switches sides when he realises he's on the losing side or the gritty private who has to fend off attacks and dangers as they arise? Tricky one, eh – well in the world of business, it's the first lot who habitually get lauded and applauded, promoted and bonused.

The Strategic Executive defines strategy, never stopping to implement it or even to ensure that it is being implemented by anyone. He needs to be spending all his time scanning the horizon, thinking outside the box, flying kites and applying his much trumpeted business acumen to set the next game-changing initiative. He passes his "working" hours with other Strategic Executives who work for strategic partners in strategic alliances, collectively getting as much work done as a nun in a brothel.

Who cares about implementation?

Such is the pre-eminence of strategy over everything else (most notably action) then if you want to put a brake on your career or torpedo your chances in a job interview, just announce that getting things done is one of your strengths. This immediately puts you in the "not a strategic thinker" category and caps your prospects. This despite the fact that all historic great world leaders, from Caesar to Churchill, whatever their style, meticulously mastered details and coordinated tactical actions to ensure things got done.

For example Thomas Jefferson diligently and singlehandedly drafted the US Declaration of Independence by incarcerating himself in a room for three days. The modern Strategic Executive would delegate it to a middle manager and his review would comprise no more than blindly accepting all the amendments proposed by spell check. What would Microsoft Word's grammar check have made of the immortal statement, "we hold these truths to be self-evident that all men are created equal, that they are endowed by their Creator with certain inalienable rights, that among these are life, liberty and the pursuit of happiness"? Far too long. Green-line treatment. Why can't we say something like, "We are aliens who are very happy when in the pursuit of life and liberty"?

Not long after Jefferson's literary masterpiece, history started to change sides. In 1815 the greatest military *strategist* of all-time, Napoleon, was defeated by the greatest military *tactician* of all-time, the Duke of Wellington. Ever since, bit by bit, strategising has recovered. Execution given way to excrement.

And so now, in today's world of business bullshit, the ability to implement counts for less. The name of the game is waffling away about organisational excellence, scalable models, partner enablement, leading at the higher level, continuous improvement and agile decision-making. It's always sobering to recall that breathing, eating and sleeping are all tactical actions; grandstanding is strategic.

BRITISH HISTORY WOULD HAVE BEEN VERY DIFFERENT IF STRATEGIC EXECUTIVES HAD BEEN INVENTED SOONER

But the Strategic Executive is not going to go away – quite the opposite. Business schools and business books are encouraging these guys to proliferate. Students who don't think they'll be able to make it as "celebrities" are pouncing on this alternative way of becoming an overpaid good-for-nothing. So we need to redress and undress all this nonsense. And where better to start than a Day in the Life of a Strategic Executive?

II

WELCOME TO HIS WORLD – A DAY IN THE LIFE OF A STRATEGIC EXECUTIVE

This chapter follows a day in the life of the Strategic Executive, embracing new technologies like smart 'phones, webinars, cloud computing and I-pads as much he eschews traditional techniques like turning up on time and knowing the names of his fellow employees.

It is actually difficult to pinpoint the starting point of a Strategic Executive's day since in some senses he never finishes work from the previous day. Armed with his BlackBerry, his vacuous emissions can continue all night, serving no other purpose than to indicate that his life has been taken over by the need to be seen to be available "24/7".

But for the sake of convention, let's assume that the Strategic Executive's working day starts when he leaves home (or the hotel he unnecessarily stayed in) and drives to work (Strategic Executives never use public transport). The Strategic Executive drives to work in his company 4x4, a vehicle capable of driving off-road in a South American jungle but which spends its time on the rugged outback that is the M4. Nevertheless its ludicrously disproportionate over-size wheels give its driver that extra height, which in his mind is a fair reflection of his standing and status in the business world. To everyone else he looks like a tosser.

DRIVING OUTSIDE THE BOX

Rather than do anything cultured or informative like listen to Radio 4's "Today" programme or some decent music, the Strategic Executive irritates his colleagues by randomly 'phoning them on his inaudible bluetooth, asking inane questions competing with the noise of the traffic and not paying the slightest attention to their answers. He calls it, "keeping them on their toes"; they call it, "getting on my tits."

The eagle has landed

And so, after carelessly parking his car such that it straddles two parking spaces, our hero arrives in his salubrious office with its name plate (easily replaced, in case they need to "let him go"). The personal office is *the* great and still thriving flagship of business bullshit. Despite all the management-speak rhetoric of collaboration, team-working, cross-functional project teams and flat hierarchies, bosses *still* have their own offices. Where in any business book does anyone dare say that hiding the leader away from his team in an over-furnished, remote and spacious area, ostentatiously marking out his higher salary and status makes any business sense?

Having breezily asked his PA, "nice weekend?" – a curious greeting for a Wednesday morning – the Strategic Executive settles down in his Big Brother diary room chair to see what the day holds in store for him. His organisational skills are so poor that every scheduled meeting comes as a complete surprise to him, although he has perfected the art of pretending that he has read the briefing papers circulated for the meeting.

Having logged in (using the only password he can remember, "password") he sends out a few e-mails but his over-reliance on spellcheck combined with the fact that his chubby fingers are about as targeted as a dirty cluster bomb means that these early morning forays into literature generally cause confusion and mayhem. For instance his stab at encouraging meaningful introspection degenerates into a common belief that he would like everyone to go fishing as his attempt at "soul searching" produces "sole searching". Not that it really matters because it's all a load of codswallop anyway.

Although he doesn't know it, this is his day

9.00 a.m. KPM review meeting

11.00 a.m. Appraisal meeting with Business Development Manager

12.00 noon Lunch with John Uppisarce, Strategic Executive, BAI Bank plc

2.00 p.m.   Conference call with various hangers-on

4.00 p.m.   Leaver's presentation

9.00 a.m. KPM review meeting

KPM stands for "key performance measures", since just as politicians now only make "keynote" speeches and no longer mere speeches, all indicators are "key" and there are no such things as plain old "performance measures."

The KPM meeting affords the first encounter of the day with the dreaded PowerPoint presentation. "Death by PowerPoint" has become a standing joke in business but is somewhat unfair to PowerPoint since there are no independently verified recorded instances of people actually *dying* from sitting through such a presentation. That said, *"coma* by PowerPoint" is quite commonplace and "yawn-a-long-a-PowerPoint" more or less compulsory.

How different history would have been if PowerPoint had been invented a few centuries earlier. Instead of Martin Luther King's "I have a dream" speech he could have transmitted a massive series of slides headed, "Images I experienced whilst asleep". And Winston Churchill's World War II gravelly radio broadcasts were all very well but wouldn't they have been so much more effective if everyone could have sat in front of their computer watching slides entitled "Locations for fighting them," "What I can offer you" and "De-briefing on recent events in the field of human conflict"?

Also Nelson's great pre-Battle of Trafalgar message, "England expects every man to do his duty," was just made for PowerPoint. The flags would have been hoisted in bullet-point format proudly proclaiming:

Expectations

- **Country of origin**

- **Talent Pool**

- **Tasks**

- **Responsibilities**

The KPM meeting is invariably led by the Finance Director since he's the only one who understands numbers. Unfortunately for his career prospects, numbers are about the *only* thing he understands. Amongst the more obvious gaps in his knowledge are humour, words and interacting with fellow human beings.

Finance Directors are a strange breed whose principal survival technique revolves around the fact that nobody can spot any of their technical bluffs which they habitually use to deflect ideas they don't like or, more often, *people* they don't like. After all, who's going to argue with an FD when he says, "there are tax efficient ways for not doing it like that," "this is a Companies Act requirement" or the ultimate threat to their boss, "Post Sarbanes Oxley, as the chief executive, you could go to prison over this." In the US, Finance Directors are known as CFOs which they claim to be an abbreviation for Chief Finance Officer although the suspicion remains that it stands for something more coarse.

Typically the KPM meeting will comprise a review of between 20 and 100 "key" performance measures, of which the Strategic Executive understands two. He skilfully disguises his ignorance by nodding knowledgeably when people whom he perceives to be respected speak and bolting out of the room whenever his BlackBerry rings. He will ask the occasional daft question, which his subordinates impute with more intelligence than it merits and therefore provide the answer to a more sophisticated version of the question. This totally bamboozles the Strategic Executive who nevertheless considers his mission accomplished by virtue of the fact that he appears to have stimulated an intelligent debate.

Personal business

To universal relief, the KPM meeting ends and the Strategic Executive, blissfully ignorant of his next planned appointment, retreats to his lair, like a taxi to its rank, in order to await the next person to hail him down. Whilst waiting, he speedily follows up some "top of mind" issues. Like a packet of crisps.

With the attention span of a retarded turkey, the last thing he would do is methodically analyse his in-tray and assign priorities. For the Strategic Executive, such efficiency is something to be spoken of but never done. Instead he receives a call from his supervisor (legally known as his wife) who reminds him that he needs to sort out the insurance claim for the damage to next door's greenhouse caused by their obnoxious brat's over-exuberant use of the latest must-have gimmick for middle-class show-offs, Wii haggis throwing.

Then he has a shock. The Strategic Executive is catapulted into the real world of business by assuming the role of customer to some other Strategic Executive's organisation. He is required to 'phone a call centre. Call centres are aptly named – they are not described as "answer centres" or "response centres" let alone "satisfactory solution centres", they are just "call centres."

Call centres present a number of challenges to anyone (remembering your password, keeping your sanity and trying to disguise the fact that you're making an extended personal call when you should be working, to name but three). The greatest challenge of all is, of course, trying to speak to a human. There are plenty of near misses:

- "Your call is important to us – so important, in fact, that we have diverted it to a call centre in the cheapest part of the world – linked by Third World technology – and staffed by inadequately trained people who barely speak English."

- "All our consultants are busy serving other customers at the moment but your call will be answered shortly as soon as an overworked operator becomes available, having finished annoying the previous valuable caller."

Eventually you do get through to a human who *fortunately* has been extensively trained but *unfortunately* intensively trained in only one thing, i.e. how to calm down irate callers and get them off the line without addressing their underlying problem.

11.00 a.m. Appraisal meeting with Business Development Manager

This frustration abruptly ends when a pop-up window on the Strategic Executive's screen interrupts his viewing of Asian Babes.com to inform him that he has a meeting scheduled with one of his direct reports, the Business Development Manager.

A STRATEGIC EXECUTIVE GETS A TASTE OF HIS OWN MEDICINE

As it happens, the meeting is a mid-year review and has been planned and in the Strategic Executive's diary for six months. For all these reasons the meeting is inevitably cancelled and replaced by a request that the appraisee complete a "self-appraisal." This grotesque and rude abdication of responsibility on the part of the Strategic Executive is held out as a great example of "employee empowerment." More like "employer idleness".

To be fair to the Strategic Executive, however, an appraisal meeting with a Business Development manager is Meeting Impossible because whatever it is that people in business development or marketing do, it's completely unmeasurable. As a veteran Managing Director once said of his longstanding Director of Marketing Communications, "Nice bloke – I haven't a clue what he does for a living."

12 noon: Business lunch

Business lunches fall into 2 categories - those that achieve next to nothing and those that achieve absolutely nothing. They usually comprise one of two combinations of participants, i.e. people who already have a business relationship which is not going to change as a consequence of the meal or a couple of blokes who have no hope of securing a deal but fancy a freebee lunch.

It is generally held that when British people meet, they enter into an inane conversation about the weather. This does not, however, apply in business circles where they invariably enter into inane speculation about the state of the economy. One lesson which bullshitters learn early on is that you should never talk about the past. Facts have an inconvenient tendency of contradicting you. It's a different game when you talk about the future because nobody can disprove what you say. Thus whilst one Strategic Executive tries to puzzle out which item of cutlery he should select from the bewildering array on the table before him, the other trots out a series of Mystic Meg predictions for interest rate movements, GDP growth and how China's going to rule the World.

The start of all this drivel is always accompanied by conspicuous ordering of sparkling water. Strategic Executives know that first impressions count so their tactic here is to appear to be a responsible, cost-conscious teetotaller before going on to drink copious amounts of expensive wine for the remainder of the meal.

2.00 p.m. Conference call

Duly stuffed and tanked up, the Strategic Executive returns for the ultimate challenge of his day: staying awake for the duration of an afternoon conference call, when – after his ample lunch - the old body clock is saying, "sleeeeeep, you are tired and fat."

The conference call is one great product of the relentless march of technology and enables groups of people at remote locations to "listen" to each other, in the way that we listen to shopping mall musak. This great apotheosis of tedium has culminated in the total yawn-in which is "webinars." A hideous technological setback enabling you to see a PowerPoint presentation taking place thousands of miles away. Technology may be making the world a smaller place: it's also making it one enormous dormitory.

The webinar has taken "coma by PowerPoint" to a new level since it removes the physical presence of the speaker from the equation. This deprives listeners of the stimulation of observing the idiosyncratic mannerisms of the speakers. The audience is confronted solely by the soporific reality of the presentation slides. Churchgoing may very well be in decline but it's not because once a week people can't bear an hour's tedious, tendentious and repetitive chanting presided over by an implausibly cheerful bloke in funny clothes. It's because they've

THE ART OF CONFERENCE CALL PARTICIPATION IS TO DIS-
GUISE ONE'S WHEREABOUTS AND
INACTIVITY

already had five days of it at work.

The main activity of a conference call revolves around the use of the "mute" button, i.e. the button which enables the "participants" at any given location to elect to listen but not be heard. Designed to stop unnecessary background noise from the various audience locations interfering with the speaker's presentation, this button is a godsend since it enables those not presenting to chat amongst themselves. The challenge, however, is to spot the time to cut off from chatting amongst yourselves and rejoin the yawn-in when asked a question or for a comment. This is easier said than done so easily the most commonly heard statement during a conference call is, "sorry I didn't quite catch that, it's a bit of a bad line."

Oh, and one fundamental tip regarding the mute button: if you want to totally sabotage your career prospects, get confused between when the mute button is on and when it is off. This will not only ensure that your boss's question is met with complete silence but that his beautifully crafted presentation will be accompanied by your running commentary with such pearls of wisdom as "God, this is dull," "he really hasn't got a clue" and, "is it true that he's screwing Stephanie in Accounts?"

The ultimate absurdity of the conference call is when both ends of the line are on mute. This happens when the listeners, having asked a question and not being the least bit interested in the answer, revert to chatting amongst themselves whilst the presenters work out amongst themselves which one of them is going to answer. You can't help but wonder whether or not Alexander Graham Bell would have bothered patenting his "apparatus for transmitting vocal sounds telegraphically," if he'd known it would all come to this. It's good to talk: it's just that sometimes it's a lot better to go on mute.

Apart from staying awake, the great challenge of a conference call is what to look at. Basically you have a group of people sitting round a table staring at a telephone. It's not going to last. So, after about 30 seconds, the sideway glances, the surreptitious scrutiny of each other's appearance and the whole process of mentally undressing your colleagues begin. Well, at least this keeps you awake.

On this particular call, the Strategic Executive has at least managed to avoid another great pitfall of conference calls, namely that of attending the wrong call. With the proliferation of conference calls, the haphazard and careless way people arrange them and distribute conference call numbers and their unique PIN numbers, it is quite easy to stumble into the wrong call.

To make matters worse, given that the waffle to be heard is difficult to differentiate from one call to another, it is not immediately clear that you've landed in the wrong place. In fact the previous sentence holds true even if you replace the words "not immediately" with "never". There ought to be a word for this. So, if absenteeism is the act of *deliberately* avoiding something deadly dull, then how about calling it presenteeism? The act of *accidentally* turning up at something deadly dull. Remember where you heard this first: it'll be in the next edition of the OED.

Anyway presenteeism need not be a career-blocker since all conference calls are basically the same (the organiser is boasting about his latest project). Therefore there are a few sure-fire "contributions" which will work in all calls. If you're ever lost for words, just try, "I think this is a great insight into a business-critical issue," or, "this has really motivated me to look into how we can incorporate the ideas we've heard today into what we will be doing tomorrow." Works every time.

THE OMISSION OF THE WORD "OFF" AT THE END OF A SENTENCE CAN HAVE UNINTENDED EFFECTS ON ITS MEANING

4.00 p.m. Leaver's presentation

And so the Strategic Executive manages to survive the yawn-in without more than a couple people noticing he'd dropped off. Reawakened and still not entirely sure what day it is, he is mildly alarmed to be informed that he is due to make the speech marking the last day of Ceri in Customer Services. Problem is – he hasn't a clue who Ceri is but really hopes it's not the one he embarrassed himself with at the Christmas party. He asks his immediate cronies for a few funny stories, which he then muddles up in a speech notable only for its convincing pretence of his being Ceri's lifelong friend and mentor. "A great speech," he says afterwards.

Unlike the Strategic Executive, Ceri has had ample time to prepare a speech to mark her departure but behaves as if she too has only just been informed that she needs to speak. In a toe-curling, excruciatingly embarrassed style she manages to mutter out the obligatory leaving speech mantra that, "the people here are the best thing about this company," and implores them to, "stay in touch." Safe in the knowledge that within a few hours, she'll never see any of them again.

So another "working" day draws to a close. At this stage that the Strategic Executive waddles back to his den and for the first time in the day suddenly appears busy. This is because he knows that a number of people will leave in about five minutes' time and he needs to impress them by appearing to be in for a long evening's work. Suddenly he strikes up conversation with people he's ignored all day. "Have a nice evening; I'm not sure when I'll be getting away myself." Once they've gone, he pings off a few more of his trademark, arse-covering e-mails and skedaddles off for a bit of road rage and nose-picking on the way home.

This routine or variations of it is being carried across the country day in, day out by thousands of Strategic Executives. How do they get way with it? How come the World is awash with Strategic Executives? To get some idea of the answer to this conundrum, it's time to be the little boy in the crowd looking at the Emperor's new clothes and to enter into the world of mission statements, visions, business plans and all that jazz.

III

ALL THAT GLITTERS AIN'T GOLD

All pretentious activities like to give themselves a cloak of respectability by building an intellectual edifice around their inane and random activity. For instance, football, which basically comprises 22 men of low intelligence trying to kick a ball in a couple of nets, has developed a panoply of lingo around 4-4-2, metatarsals, the offside rule and so on and so forth. It even manages to provide former exponents of this great trade with a livelihood as "experts".

But the business world has taken this pseudo-intellectualism to an altogether different plane with a wide variety of mock qualifications and laughable institutions For example, there's something called the Institute of Customer Services (you just know what their call centre will be like) not to mention the Great Place to Work Institute (presumably HQ'd in Rio). You'll be disappointed to learn, however, that the Pratt Institute is not the name emerging from an unexpected flash of self-awareness on the part of the Institute of Directors but some sort of organisation for architects.

If you can bear to contain the excitement of reading the syllabus for the entrepreneurial studies qualification awarded by the Project Management Institute, then you'll get an insight into the mumbo-jumbo of the business world. It's all to do with the razzamatazz of mission statements, visions, business plans and strategic objectives.

Mission Statements

A company's mission statement is meant to encapsulate in one phrase the essence of what the business is trying to achieve in the long term.

Prima facie this is very simple: the mission of all companies is to make their rich directors and owners even richer. Unfortunately this mission statement, although having the advantage of being honest and succinct, is not the most motivational of calls to action. Therefore a whole new vocabulary of gloriously nebulous concepts such as "best-in-class," "customer preference" and "employee empowerment" etc has sprung up in the mission statement in order to disguise the company's raison d'être.

Case study of a mission statement in action: Northern Rock

Northern Rock is arguably the best example of managerial bungling buffoonery in corporate history. In 2007 it collapsed a year earlier than the other greedy and incompetent banks, having rattled up a debt to the Government (that's us, the taxpayers) of £26,900,000,000 in its ten years of existence as a listed company. So it managed to lose about £10m PER DAY!!! Let's take a look at how it held itself out to the World.

The mission statement of Northern Rock as published in its final annual report in February 2007, a mere 6 months before its pitiable collapse was:

> Northern Rock is a specialised lending and savings bank which aims to deliver superior value to customers and shareholders through excellent products, efficiency and growth.

With the benefit of hindsight, we can see that it was those words "specialised lending" which gave the game away. Northern Rock specialised in lending to people who hadn't got a cat in hell's chance of repaying them. As it turned out, however, this was quite a crowded specialism because, as became apparent a year later, HBOS, RBS, Lehman Brothers and AIG were all plunging into that particular niche.

Northern Rock's mission statement was helpfully illustrated by a little diagram entitled "The Virtuous Circle" at the top of which appeared the words "Cost Control". Note the absence of reference to gluttonous investment in dodgy sub-prime mortgages.

In case readers were not fully reassured by all these virtuous circles and soothing words, its annual report provided its readers with a nice comforting graph showing its low risk. Just as comforting as "Help the Aged" unveiling their latest advertising front-man, Dr Harold Shipman.

Vision

Corporate visions are the adult equivalent of those embarrassing primary school conversations when Sir asks, "what do you want to be when you grow up?" "An international football star, dating a popstar bimbo." As the delusion of youth gives way to the disappointment of adulthood, this puerile dream is replaced by vicarious aspirations for your own world-beating business. Only whereas your childish ambitions as a child become the subject of dinner party anecdotes, your childish ambitions as an adult are somehow taken seriously.

Of course most corporate visions are somewhere between a mirage and a fantasy but this doesn't stop people pretending to believe them. Unlike in the real world when people who have visions are thought to be religious fruitcakes, in the business world, it is considered an asset to be "visionary" and the more surreal you can be, the better your career prospects.

Strategic Objectives

A company's strategic objectives are the ways in which it will go about achieving its mission, namely the enrichment of its directors or owners. In truth strategic objectives fall into one of the following three categories:

- Make under-rewarded employees work harder;
- Make under-rewarded employees poorer; and
- Find new ways of replacing under-rewarded employees with technology and/or even poorer people in countries with cheap corporate tax regimes.

Basically there are only *two* ways of increasing profits – increasing sales or reducing costs. However the business world has, at the last count, managed to construct two *million* ways of saying this. And called them strategic objectives. Unlike the "Alice in Wonderland" world of mission statements, however, the problem with strategic objectives is that sooner or later someone needs to be seen to having implemented them. "Walk the talk," as Strategic Executives would put it. All the more difficult when most Strategic Executives do little more than squawk the squawk and stalk the cork. Never mind, let's move on.

Core values

Companies' stated core values are a needless digression into ego-massaging intended to impress readers on what jolly decent chaps the greedy bastards who run the company really are. The reality is that most companies' *real* core values are anything but edifying. If this were a Business Book, it would conjure up a corny acronym, saying that core values are BASIC, i.e.-

- Blame shifting
- Arse-licking
- Secrecy
- Indecision
- Capriciousness

Such core values – fleshed out by examples of the values in action - would make for much more entertaining reading than you find in the glossy brochures. Dream on…

Core Values of BAI plc

Blame shifting

All BAI plc staff believe passionately in the doctrine of self-infallibility. Therefore if something goes wrong, it is paramount for everyone involved to blame a colleague. The manner of blaming is equally important: finger-pointing should be done behind closed doors, down the pub after work - anything but face-to-face with the person being criticised.

Arse licking

BAI plc prides itself on having employees who are in the habit of complimenting their bosses even when they have uttered world-class absurdities and nonsensical gobbledegook. If your boss rambles incoherently in the manner of a discussion between Mad King George and David Icke, make sure you tell him what an inspirational conversation you've had.

Secrecy

BAI plc makes the Chinese Politburo look like an exemplar of the Freedom of Information Act. We empower our employees to hide, distort and deny any and all bad news. Especially concerning the bosses' whereabouts on a Friday afternoon.

Indecision

At BAI plc we are continuously looking for new and innovative ways of avoiding taking decisions. Only when a sufficient number of senior Strategic Executives have openly backed an idea, will our middle managers get off the fence and provide their whole-hearted endorsement.

Capriciousness

In our tireless quest for operational excellence at BAI plc, we believe in taking whimsical decisions based on a mixture of prejudice, stupidity and petulance.

Back to the real World

Alas the number one rule of business literature is to avoid such candour and make the crap they churn out as dull and predictable as a Parkinson interview. And thus we come up against the more conventional core values, such as

> Integrity
>
> People who boast about their integrity don't possess it. Should have been a Chinese proverb.
>
> Customer Focus
>
> If businesses really did prioritise customer needs and "put the customer first", they would of course go bust very quickly because ultimately the customer wants to pay as little as possible for as much as possible.
>
> Innovation
>
> Another favourite word in the Strategic Executives lexicon. And to be fair to them, they're always finding new and innovative ways of avoiding tax, justifying boardroom pay and covertly maximising their leisure time.
>
> Service
>
> Strategic Executives increasingly are following the lead of politicians who purport to "serve" their constituents. The sort of service they have in mind is of the self-service variety, e.g. helping themselves to bigger bonuses.

Bringing it all together

"He has some dreams, which he calls plans," Benjamin Disraeli

Mission statements, objectives, core values and other business bullshit are forced into a "Business plan" which is a remarkably soporific and poorly written document earning its just deserves by being read in full by absolutely nobody, including its various writers. It is therefore judged by its size and how pretty the cover looks.

It is important that the Strategic Executive never spends too much time on any detailed work so reading a business plan for which they are notionally responsible is completely out of the question. They will, however, *say* that they have read it on the basis that they have perused the so-called "executive summary". Why is it called an "executive summary" as opposed to a mere "summary"? Is it because only Strategic Executives have the brain power to fully grasp the essence of a long document from an abridged introduction? Or is it in fact quite the opposite - like a news bulletin on Five News, it makes a point of avoiding the use of long words and ignoring any complicated issues, which require some sort of background knowledge?

But despite appearances, all this drivel isn't conjured up effortlessly and given that senior management has more important things to do than deal with detail, it takes the business world's equivalent of the State Opening of Parliament (an annual ceremony for no apparent purpose, complete with people performing bizarre rituals in silly costumes) to kick-start this nonsense. This is the jolly that is the Business Planning Away Day.

The Business Planning Away Day is like one of those "EastEnders" specials filmed on Clacton Pier: they comprise the same old rubbish, just different scenery at a different location. It is a mechanism whereby top-level executives, who can't bear the thought of spending time with grubby middle managers, lessen the blow by wasting money on a day out in a remote luxury country hotel. Really badly run companies will organise longer trips to more luxurious places further afield but the result is the same. Now sometimes referred to as summits, retreats or even symposiums (ancient Greek for piss-up), they have evolved a comedic routine all of their own.

The planned agenda (usually published by a stressed out PA after everyone's already left work the day before the start) is something like:

Time	Item
8.30 a.m.	Coffee and welcome
9.30 a.m.	Introductions
10.00 a.m.	Scene setting
10.45 a.m.	Coffee
11.00 a.m.	Objectives for break-out session
12 noon	Working Lunch
12.30 p.m.	Break-out Sessions
3.00 p.m.	Tea
3.30 p.m.	Feedback from break-out sessions
4.30 p.m.	Wrap-up/Future actions

Actual agenda

Time	"Activity"
8.30 a.m.	Mad rush for free bacon sarnies and croissants at 9.25; boss avoidance; chat with your mates.
9.30 a.m.	Meeting commences with everyone getting out their laptop and completely ignoring the proceedings. Superfluous and embarrassed introductions since everyone knows each other anyway.
10.30 a.m.	Trumpet-blowing introduction by CEO making use of an out-of-date and only vaguely relevant PowerPoint presentation he made to the company's bankers a few months ago.
11.00 a.m.	Extended coffee break in which everyone becomes intensely interested in messages left on their mobiles and makes every effort to make a wide variety of superfluous calls in a bid to appear important, busy and indispensable.
11.30 a.m.	Rambling and uncontrolled discussion about nothing in particular, hijacked by office whinger, complaining about the fact that nobody's done anything about the air conditioning vent above her desk being too draughty.
12 noon	In a truly pathetic attempt to disguise the fact that Away Days are jollies, it is important that the lunch break is timetabled as brief and working. Away Day lunches are in reality always both leisurely and prolonged as a consequence of a combination of the universal desire not to return to the meeting, the confusing instructions as to where lunch is to be taken and the general obsession with unnecessary mobile 'phone calls.

Time	"Activity"
1.55 p.m.	CEO leaves for unexpected round of golf, leaving the Business Development Director suddenly finding himself the unexpected and ill-deserved centre of attention (Clegg Syndrome).
2 p.m. (or 14:00 p.m. as it is known in the semi-literate business world)	Break-out sessions – 25 minutes spent finding a room, nominating a chairman and scribe; next hour and a half spent "brainstorming." What a wonderful concept brainstorming is. You'd think it was a combination of Frank "think the unthinkable" Field and Monty Python coming together in the business world, as great titanic intellectual colossuses dig deep into their business experience to produce earth-shattering ideas which will change the whole course of corporate history. In fact it comprises everyone looking embarrassed except for the Strategic Executive who seizes the opportunity to ingratiate himself with senior management by regurgitating ideas he's heard his bosses espouse, however fanciful and ridiculous. Last five minutes spent scribbling half-baked ideas on a flipchart.
4.00 p.m.	Repeat of morning coffee break, only with tea and more flatulence.
4.45 p.m.	Break-out sessions feedback totally ignored (or "parked" as it is known), i.e. facilitator gives instruction for flipcharts to be collected by CEO's PA who subsequently leaves them in her boyfriend's car which she has borrowed for the day. (Everyone is so uninspired by the contents that a conspiracy of silence envelopes their existence).

The all-time list of completed action points resulting from Business Planning Away Days

.

Business Plans: the aftermath

Business Planning Away Days are a monumental waste of time and money. They are often held on Fridays, which allows a little extra time (i.e. during the immediately following weekend) to make sure everyone completely forgets any good intentions or insightful ideas they came across. The business carries on as if the Away Day had never happened.

The Business Plan itself has an equally pathetic after-life. It is usually redundant by Day 1 of the year it purports to describe and has anyone anywhere ever referred to a Business Plan from a previous year? Are they ever kept? They basically have the life expectancy of one of Jordan's marriages and are about as likely to describe future events as King Harold II's little known chef d'oeuvre, "My plans for 1067".

What a pity that the same fate doesn't befall the most sinister departments of them all: HR.

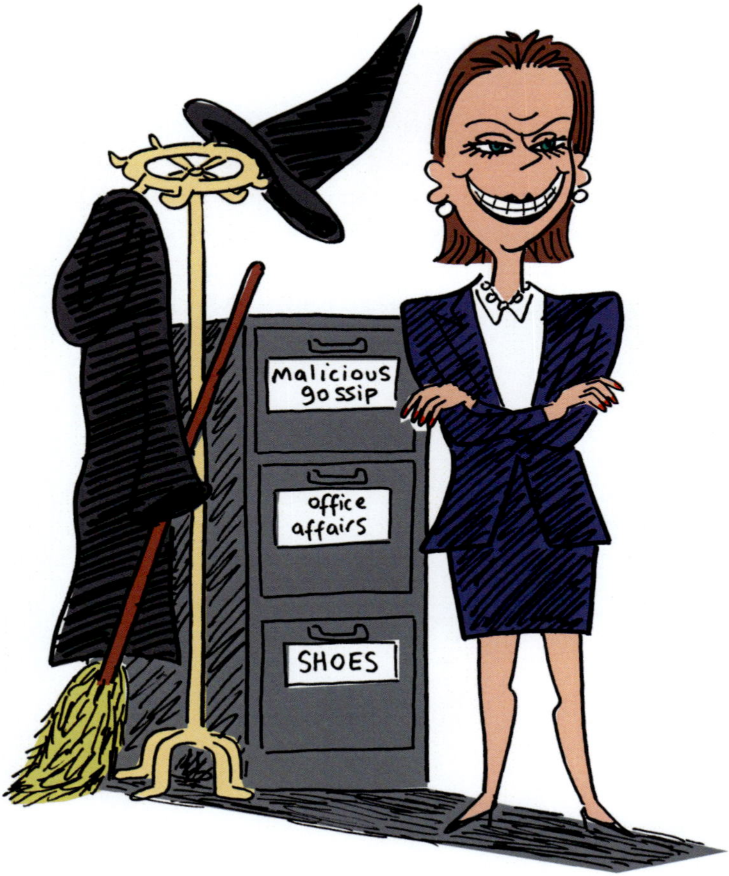
Malicious gossip
office affairs
SHOES

IV

AWAY WITH THE FAIRIES - THE SELF-DELUSIONAL WORLD OF PERSONNEL

In May 1994, under the headline "Personnel Officers are a waste of time", "The Independent" reported the conclusions of a London School of Economics report which showed that companies without a personnel function did just as well as those that had them. And yet somehow this species survives, albeit now re-branded in line with other sinister viral strains beginning with the letter H. Thus in addition to HIV (aids) and H1N1 (pig flu), we now have HR (office superbug).

Unlike other departments, the HR "team" (in fact, they're more like a coven) has no intrinsic subject-matter expertise, so for their power and influence they rely entirely on sucking up to the bosses and snitching on staff. And yet their outward persona is one of friendliness and support to all employees. And to whom do these airheads owe their survival? Meet the Ice Queen, the Head of HR. Here's a poem that the Poet Laureate may have written about her. And by "poem", I mean normal prose, with dubious punctuation, not making full use of the width of the page.

Her hair is impeccable
Her laugh inscrutable
Her stare withering
Her sting fatal.
Her heart is unfathomable
Her sense of humour sadistic
Rarely is she seen performing normal human functions
Like eating, sleeping or crying
She never coughs, sneezes or yawns.
But she smiles.
Like Hannibal Lecter.
She smiles.

Like the Queen bee surrounded by her mindless workers, the Ice Queen works serenely behind bullet-proof glass and is transported around the country in a refrigerated van, in order to avoid the double risks of assassination and melting. And like the Queen of England, the Ice Queen's rare interactions with "normal" people are forced conversations on a regal walkabout.

The Ice Queen functions like a nuclear deterrent. Everyone thinks they need one because everyone else has got one but in fact they are expensive to maintain, thoroughly odious and no use to anyone. The fact that they have survived is down to a number of factors, one of which is that they protect the business from the dreaded "Employee Tribunal", which they depict as a grotesquely unreasonable bunch of vindictive buffoons, dishing out "unlimited fines" to companies for their honest attempts to get rid of recalcitrant employees. In fact according to the 2011/12 report of the Orwellian-sounding Ministry of Justice, only 8% of the unfair dismissal claims "disposed of" in that period resulted in compensation being awarded and the average award was around £5k.

So if the price of liberating your business from HR is just the occasional five grand fine, wouldn't you say that's a real bargain?

Unlike the Ice Queen herself, her busy entourage have all the right qualities to be children's TV presenters – an impossibly cheerful demeanour, a superficial understanding of everything they talk about and a patronising way of conversing with everyone they meet. Many of them even struggle to spell their own names, which have an irritating habit of ending in "-ii": Debbii, Dannii, Caitii, Siouxsii and co. They often have job titles such as "HR specialist", a flawed concept since there's nothing of substance to specialise in. They might as well call themselves Breathing Specialists.

In so far as it is possible to construct a raison d'être for their existence, the Ice Queen has managed to style HR as "business partners", sometimes even aspiring to such emetic expressions as the "conscience and soul" of the organisation. To the extent that it is possible to make sense of their self-aggrandising claptrap, the core functions of this crew appear to be to "Recruit, train and retain." Let's see what they really mean by these terms.

Excuse No.1 for the existence of HR: Recruitment

Behind croneyism and nepotism, the most common recruitment technique is the job interview. And yet the absolute worst way to work out a candidate's suitability must be to have a chat with them. Charming bullshitters (like Bernard Madoff, Chris Huhne and Stuart Hall), flirty females or well-rehearsed actors will all sail through whereas people who exhibit rare but invaluable characteristics such as self-awareness, humility and self-deprecation fall by the wayside.

Sometimes I act on Sheer business acumen. No need for an interview or references for this one. Mr. Ripper from Whitechapel Starts in Ladieswear first thing monday.

As if this method of recruiting wasn't ridiculous enough, the HR team manages to make matters much worse by weeding out the best candidates before the interview stage. This they do by way of "screening" job applications, using their insight into bugger-all to randomly select the people for interview. They will skilfully deploy such criteria as whether or not they have ever heard of the applicant's current employer. Or whether or not the applicant shares a surname with someone they fancy off "Neighbours". At least they've learnt to turn people down in a polite manner – thus, "I reject your job application because your name sounds a bit foreign," becomes, "unfortunately due to the high volume of high calibre applicants for this position, we are unable to progress your application to the next stage."

There are, however, other more expensive and elaborate ways of recruiting the wrong people and more sophisticated Ice Queens make extensive use of these.

1.   Psychometric tests

Nowadays most people rejoice in the diversity and multiculturalism of our cosmopolitan world. Not so HR who love nothing better than labelling people and putting them in pigeonholes – although never more than four because anything higher is a big, scary number if you're an HR specialist. And their pigeonhole tendencies start at the recruitment stage, with some good old psychometric testing.

This is where HR meets astrology, categorising people by reference to some Mickey Mouse classifications, a bit like those naff quizzes you do in newspapers. It doesn't seem to occur to what passes for the HR intelligentsia that people will answer the questions in such a way as to impress or that they'll notice after three questions, that the best option is always C or that the numbers in brackets give away the scoring system.

Anyway, see how you fare in this challenging quiz: if you get a good score, the prize is a job in HR....

Q1: Which of the following best describes how you would handle the delicate issue of a female colleague with body odour?
a) I'd say to her, "hey darling, I bet you're really struggling to get a man these days." (0.5)
b) I'd buy her a bunch of flowers, chuck some cheap perfume at her and try it on with her. (1)
c) I'd refer to HR procedure ACN 0456, "Handling delicate and sensitive subjects in a compassionate but fair and firm way." (100)

Q2: Rank the following in order of likelihood:
a) Cabinet minister enjoying the Prime Minister's "full support" to keep his job for one week.
b) France to award UK 12 points in Eurovision Song Contest.
c) Flying pig to pass over England beating Germany in a penalty shoot-out.
d) Employee appeal against company disciplinary action to be upheld.

Q3: As an HR professional, how would you describe Anders Brievik, the Norwegian loon who massacred 67 students?
a) Someone in need of a training needs analysis.
b) Someone who should submit a formal grievance concerning the challenges he faces with upper management in accordance with procedure ACN 6933.
c) Someone in a redundancy pool.
d) An evil bastard.

So how did you score?

Points	Description
200 to 300	Congratulations, you've shown just the sort of commitment to petty, bureaucratic procedures which are gradually driving commonsense from the workplace. You're one of us!
100 to 199	You're real Strategic Executive material with your helicopter view of things – you make a great deal of noise, are completely detached and totally unable to affect what's happening on the ground.
25 to 99	In HR parlance, we've identified an area to focus on strengthening. It's called humanity.
Less than 25	Mathematically impossible to get this score but HR people can't count

2   Assessment centres

Just as Plato's "Republic" basically concludes that the republic should be run by people just like Plato, then so recruitment assessment centres inevitably arrive at the conclusion that successful applicants should be people just like the people who run them. They are in fact run by middle-aged management consultants trying to cash in on gullible HR functions with too big a budget. Surprise, surprise - they invariably result in recommendations to recruit middle aged freelance management consultant types (i.e. people whose cynicism has forced them out of real jobs and they are now temperamentally incapable of working for anyone but themselves).

Meanwhile the best basis for a recruitment decision, i.e. taking a reference in order to speak to someone who has actually worked with the applicants, is relegated to being an afterthought in the process. Bizarrely this often happens once the job offer letter has been sent and accepted. It's not so much closing the stable door after the horse has bolted, as not bothering to check whether or not the horse is a Tyrannosaurus Rex until just after you've let it into the kindergarten play area.

But so far we have only focused on in-house HR people. Outside, however, a much more cretinous breed lurks...

3 Recruitment agents

In all the best horror movie thrillers, the heroes escape from one horrible baddie, only to walk into the arms of something much worse. This is how it feels once you have handed your letter of resignation to one of the Ice Queen's minions and the next day turn up at a recruitment agency. There are a number of annoying things about HR recruiters, the most immediately apparent of which is their existence.

Recruitment agents and HR staff deserve each other. And they both deserve estate agents. Which reminds me about a joke – did you hear the one about the estate agent, the HR specialist and the recruitment agent who went up a hill one day? No? Nor did I, but I hope it was an active volcano. Near an approaching tsunami.

Few people can cause such instant irritation as HR recruiters manage with their absurd title references in job ads. An advert will appear in the Financial Times for the position of "CEO, BAI Bank plc (ref BS 10816)" as if the recruiter had in excess of 10,000 chief exec jobs on the go at the time and could only work out which job you were applying for by checking out the number 10,816.

Possibly the most annoying aspect of HR recruiters, however, is their two facedness. They make Silvio Berlusconi look trustworthy. On the one hand, when you deal with them as a client who might potentially give them some work, they are geniality personified. They know where you went on holiday, the name of your kids and the fact that you compromised yourself with the boss's PA at the Christmas party. They fawningly hang on to your every word, guffaw at the lamest of your jokes and remain perpetually cheerful. On the other hand when you deal with them as a job applicant, you suddenly take on the characteristics of a used condom.

When it comes to doing their jobs, their superficial nature precludes them for doing any detailed work - they don't screen (let alone read) CVs, don't stay in any one job for more than nine months (despite preaching about job stability) and forget everything. Uggh! Let's get back to the Ice Queen and her drones.

Excuse no.2 for the existence of HR: Training

Training is the second leg of the tripod (or is that triffid?) that is the HR edifice. This is mainly brought about by laughably simplistic "workshops" or sado-masochistic "computer-based training" often featuring videos with scenarios no more plausible than those to be found in porn movies and actors who failed the auditions for the local Christmas pantomime. Training courses afford Breathing Specialists another opportunity to crudely pigeonhole people into categories which reflect their Key Stage 2 worldview. "You thought you were here today to learn about leadership styles. Sorry, all I'm going to tell you is that, you're 'blue-submissive'." Much better than being "pink-useless".

Sitting-down Specialists incessantly talk about "Training Evaluation Analysis" but to date there is no independently verified instance of one ever having happened. Pity – because, if done properly, it would expose the training they recommend for the crock of shite it is.

Apart from talking to people in a condescending manner, the main purpose of training sessions is to downplay failure and gloss over incompetence. Consider Robert Green's humiliating performance in England's opening game of the 2010 World Cup when he let in a goal through his legs. The headlines on the red tops the following day, was "Hand of Clod: goalie blunder sinks England." Now imagine how that esteemed journal "HR today" would have covered the story. Beneath a headline "Employee number 16271 identifies area for development," they would have set out Robert Green's "individual development plan" comprising a Listen-with-Mother course on catching, run by a local nursery.

Training sessions

The most common form of training is a training session where a group of people with nothing in common are patronised for the day. Humans learn best over a period of time and not by cramming loads of data and techniques into one day. Most training sessions comprise 5% what you needed to know and 95% you don't (that's a made-up statistic but I bet it's right). However trainers (or facilitators as they increasingly prefer to be known, presumably since most of what they do is facile) do at least have the advantage of being entertaining, albeit in the main entirely unintentionally.

For instance, sometimes these training sessions take the name of one of the great misnomers of the business world: "masterclass". What image does this word conjure up in your mind? Mozart on music, Van Gogh on painting or Oscar Wilde on plays? Wrong! It's Jacquii from HR on "sickness leave management skills".

When we watched television footage of the North Korean politburo all mindlessly applauding Kim Jong il (or Kim Jong Dead as he is now), we smugly reassure ourselves that we would have sufficient independence of spirit to heckle, boo or conspicuously not stand up to sing the national anthem. So, if we are so free-spitited, why do we always respond to the question at the end of the training session, "have your objectives for today been achieved?" by moronically say, "yes, my expectations have been exceeded"?

This ritual forms part of the round robin questioning when the facilitator (an external consultant with a vested interest in prolonging the training session in order to maximise his fees) asks the same question to all 27 people in the room. Nobody listens to the people who speak before them because they're trying to work out what to say when it's their turn and nobody listens to anyone afterwards because they're bored shitless.

In some cases, the facilitators manage to justify an even larger fee by spinning the training out over multiple days. An intrinsic part of this filibustering is to waste the first hour or so of any given day by starting it with a review of the activity and "lessons learnt" from the previous day. Imagine how you'd feel if, when standing on a cold winter's morning on Platform 92 at Clapham Junction, the public address system suddenly announced, "Ding dong - the 7.20 train to Reading is running late whilst the driver reflects upon his lessons learnt from his journeys yesterday."

In fact with incontinent BlackBerries ringing, facilitators flogging their wares and padding out the time, the whole experience is so stuffed with reviews, previews, adverts and telephone numbers and so devoid of actual original content that it starts to resemble an episode of "I'm a celebrity, get me out of here". Except that a more appropriate title would be "I'm a human, how the hell did I get in here".

Excuse No.3 for the existence of HR: Retention

Retention is another key component of the HR house of cards. What they mean by this is *staff* retention whereas we all know that it is only in the sphere of *anal* retention (in respect of their own procedures) that HR has any ability. HR's approach to retention starts with the induction process where on Day 1 of your new job you are required to remember the names and roles of 121 people you are fleetingly introduced to plus forced to read what you take to be the dullest literary creation of all-time, the Staff Handbook. This conviction is rapidly shattered when, on

Day 2, the Office Procedures Manual makes its first appearance.

One of the tools for retention is the away-day team-bonding session. The idea is that if everyone spends a day on an assault course, then somehow they'll all work better together once they're back in the office. This idea was handsomely disproved in World War I when both sides played football for a day in Christmas 1914 and then spent the next four years heartily shooting the hell out of each other.

HR do, however, have quite a key role in the opposite of retention, i.e. "terminations." "Terminations" is a bizarre euphemism in that it actually sounds more terrifying than the word it is trying to ameliorate, namely dismissals. A termination sounds pretty final, if not fatal, and you have to wonder how long it'll be before they graduate to referring to "exterminations".

Discipline in the HR household

In reality the Ice Queen and her cronies' approach to *retention* is to make it feel more like *detention* and so disciplinary and grievance procedures take centre stage in their Bible of Bureaucracy, known as the Staff Handbook.

Unfortunately in the sphere of discipline, HR specialists have wheedled their way into the echelons of law-making, so the old fashioned way of sitting down with a failing employee and saying, "things are not working out, let's come to an agreement on a severance package," are passé. In their place we have the protracted charade of the disciplinary process. This usually results in the same outcome but takes ten times as long, costs several dozen times as much and en route helps justify the existence of the HR function. I wonder if this is how the Ice Queen operates at home…

Monday
Enter stage left, spoilt brat who willfully smashes a vase.
Enter stage right, Mummy Ice Queen, smiling, who starts to write a letter.
Tuesday
Mummy Ice Queen, grinning, presents letter to brat.
"Dear Rupert
I am writing to invite you to a disciplinary hearing to be held in "Orangerie" (Room A1076) before I leave for work tomorrow morning at 5.45 a.m. The purpose of the meeting is to discuss areas of concern surrounding your lack of attention to detail when walking past fragile and valuable objects. You may be accompanied by a trade union representative.
Yours sincerely
Mummy (the one who only plays with you with the camcorder's on)"

Wednesday

Enter stage left, brat - spraying graffiti on the walls and uttering obscenities at a passing grandmother. Accompanied by Bob Crowe.

Mummy Ice Queen: "As you know this meeting has been convened to discuss areas for concern relating to your lack of attention to detail when in the vicinity of delicate objects. I have conducted a survey of all household members run by the independent market researchers Kangaroo Court and it shows that 110% of those surveyed expressed total agreement with the statement, "I completely utterly irrevocably agree that Rupert's behaviour warrants formal disciplinary action." What do you have to say about that?"

Bob Crowe: "My member has been the victim of ageist discrimination and on the basis of the Politically Correct Over-the-Top Act 2009 will be initiating action for constructive dismissal. This is supported by the fact that, whereas you tolerate imbecility, drunkenness and clumsiness on the part of a 44 year old male member of the household, my member is being publicly rebuked for behaviour of a far less serious nature. Furthermore the treatment of my member has been the cause of considerable stress for him and he has been signed off work for two months by Dr Sicknote."

Mummy Ice Queen: "Thank you for coming today and for your comments, which will be faithfully noted in the official minutes which I wrote earlier. We'll be in touch."

Brat and Bob Crowe depart. Mummy Ice Queen writes letter.

Thursday
Mummy Ice Queen presents following letter to brat.

"Dear Piers

Further to our meeting yesterday, I have referred your comments concerning your alleged inappropriate behaviour to the management team of Banana Republic Ltd. After careful consideration, we have chosen to totally disregard them.

We wish to develop a Corrective Action Plan and will assess your progress in six weeks' time."

Friday
Office explodes, killing everyone except Mummy Ice Queen who is incarcerated in her maximum-security, steel and concrete reinforced office-cum-bunker.

Saturday
Mummy Ice Queen writes following article for in-house magazine.

"Hi everyone
What a week we've had! The office relocation project has been fast-tracked and those of you who have been commenting that the air-conditioning's been struggling to keep the office warm during the recent cold snap will have been pleasantly surprised at 3.15 p.m. on Friday. We also rolled out our new "How to arrange things on your Desk" procedure and it's gone off with a bang.
Keep on adding value
Alisoniii"

The unanswered question

If I were to launch a new range of "T"-shirts, it would comprise a picture of an executive's door with the name badge "HR department." Underneath would appear the word, "why?"

Shudder. Let's leave the Ice Queen in her igloo and get back to something we spend most of our working life doing – covering up the fact that we haven't done our job properly.

V

OFFICE-GATE: THE GREAT OFFICE FARCE COVER-UP

This book is not intended to be a career self-help guide but here are some tips on how you can enhance your career progression by fully engaging in the great charade which is the business world. Apart from the fundamentals (such as never admit a mistake, set outrageous deadlines and promise to achieve equally absurd ones inflicted upon you in the hope that they'll be quickly forgotten), there are some more subtle techniques which it is essential to master, if you intend to climb the greasy pole. And none of them have got anything to do with doing a good job. Quite the opposite in fact. Most of the time we produce work which, on merit, should take its rightful place in a Scoop-a-Poop park bin. However, Oliver Letwin's not always on hand to help us dispose of it, so how do you disguise it? Here are a few tips:-

1. Appear sincere

Perception is reality, so you're onto a winner if you can appear sincere about any old dross. For some good examples of this, it is necessary to look beyond the business world:

- Primitive forms of pond-life are known to read "celebrity" magazines, in which people who have achieved nothing remarkable in their lives behave as if they have. Prominent amongst these is Katie Price who, having tired of naming herself after a Middle East country, is now making Henry VIII look like an expert on marital commitment.

> I always fought that bit Said 'in sickness and in Hello!'

- In the May 2010 general election, 28,228 people in the constituency of Rutland and Melton voted for Alan Duncan. This must mean that they take him seriously. Or perhaps people living in a place with such a stupid name have completely lost it.

2 Acronyms

If your work is truly crap, see if you can come up with an acronym as a label for it. Amongst the most famous of business acronyms is the notion of SMART objectives. Very clever. Very smart, in fact. Except that the A stands for achievable and the R for realistic. Don't they mean the same thing? And the M is for "measurable" whilst the S is for "specific" – how can something be measurable without being specific? Upon closer examination even this universally applied acronym is wrong – objectives should in fact just be AS. But then the size of HR departments would need to reduce by 60% so it'll never catch on.

ACRONYM RULE #1: Remember what it stands for.

3. Useful phrases

It's important to have the right vocabulary to make it in the business world. The Strategic Executive has a great lexicon in this respect. For instance he sees himself as "going the extra mile" to "raise the bar". Well he certainly has been propping up the bar very effectively and if by "going the extra mile", he means going all round the houses to get to the point, then that's also undeniably true.

So why not use a few choice phrases as cover for the underlying worthlessness of your work? The expression "legend has it" is particularly useful. Anyone reading it is aware that it is a prelude to a massive fabrication but somehow the lie sticks. For instance legend has it that Robert the Bruce was inspired to persevere fighting the English and eventually won a great battle at Bannockburn from seeing a spider rise and fall seven times in an attempt to climb up a thread of its own web. So why not try this in a business context? An application for a loan could say, "legend has it that the bank which approves this loan will get the biggest bonus in history."

Another daft expression of complete vapidity is "Blue sky thinking" – conjuring up the perception of a chain of radical ground-breaking ideas. You kind of suspect, however, that the only thought which would come to mind if you ever were to find yourself surrounded by blue sky is, "I hope the parachute works." Drawing from this head in the clouds theme, the concept of "cloud" computing has come from nowhere in recent years but anyone attending a seminar ostensibly intended to clarify what exactly this is, will come away with the conclusion that "fog" might be a more apt description.

4. It's all in the name

Unwieldy names can have a disastrous impact on success, even if the underlying product or idea is a good one. For instance two Nordic mountains should be up there among the great iconic pairings of all-time on account of their global, flight-disrupting volcanic ash emissions in the first half of 2010 and their reprise in 2011. Romulus & Remus, Laurel & Hardy, Morecambe & Wise, Hengist & Horsa and Eyjafjalljokull & Grimsvotn. Doesn't really work, does it? Solely as a consequence of the sheer unpronounceability of their names (even BBC newsreaders referred to them as the "Icelandic volcanos"), they are completely anonymous. Unlike people such as Peaches Geldof, whose name is just about the *only* memorable thing about them.

5. It's all in the appearance

It is possible to get away with presenting something absurd, if you have somehow established your credentials, got a good name or look the part. For instance the notion that all the matter in the World could be compressed into something the size of an apple is widely accepted because it comes from "Quantum Physicists" who have somehow established themselves as credible. By comparison the equally far-fetched notion that the God who created the universe happens to bear a striking resemblance to Ken Bates is dismissed because it is expounded by bearded men in dresses. Perhaps if the next Pope were called Pope Scientistus I then he might have more success convincing people about the Resurrection.

6. Desperation tactics

If all else fails, why not try the Muammar Gaddafi Guide to Survival and Success, which managed to last 42 years, the duration of most people's careers. Admittedly he was made to look respectable by visits from the likes of Toady Blair but many of his tactics you can pursue solo. You can style yourself as a Colonel, make good use of a comedy wardrobe and, when under pressure, try just about anything including claiming everyone loves you, which you can prove by marching about punching the air, surrounded by the extras from "Shaun of the Dead".

7. Business's Got Talent

An unusual option for covering up a complete absence of merit is the one often deployed on programmes like X-Factor and Britain's Got Talent. This is the sob-story revolving around a deprived background or the recent death of someone close. This tactic has not yet made it into the Business World. But for how long? One day soon the Executive Summary of a business plan will start with the words, "The chairman, founder and owner of BAI plc was bullied at school, never knew his father and supported West Ham United and yet has overcome this adversity to build a world-leading business at the cutting edge of the market it chooses to serve." You must admit that it sounds a lot better than, "I'm in charge of a pile of poo desperate for a loan."

8. Agendas

An important part of disguising the fact that you have nothing to say is constructing entire meetings where people take your crap seriously. For this it is essential to be able to prepare a meeting agenda. Just having one thing to discuss doesn't by itself warrant a meeting, so the concept of an agenda has sprung up. All agendas have no fewer than six superfluous items which surround The Only Thing to Discuss and justify the existence of the meeting. Here's a typical line-up:

```
                        BAI plc

       Agenda for meeting of the Waffle and Claptrap
                        Committee
      Date
      Location
      Attendees

           1      Apologies*
           2      Review of agenda
           3      Minutes of previous meeting
           4      Matters arising
           5      The Only Thing to Discuss
           6      Any other business
           7      Date of next meeting
```

A note here for wives of Strategic Executives: if you often wonder why your husband forgets what you tell him, it is because he is used to having an agenda laid before him with minutes of previous meetings, matters arising, etc. In this way by the time he gets round to "The Only Thing to Discuss", his brain has been galvanised into recalling what the

---

* For the uninitiated, this agenda item comes as a huge disappointment since, rather than being a rare moment of candour in the business world in which Strategic Executives apologise for the fact that they've done bugger all on the action points from the last meeting, it's just a list of people who are only "apologising" for not attending. In fact they're missing the meeting because they've forgotten it or (more likely) can't think of a decent excuse for not having done anything since the last meeting.

issue is, so that he can both a) pretend that he has remembered the issue all along and b) feign having done something about it since it was last mentioned.

9. Plagiarise

If you're ever struggling for ways to make a document longer than it need be, remember that nobody ever reads the middle bit so just cut and paste some blurb from any randomly selected internet document.

10. Market research

Another tip when it comes to making a document look impressive is that there's nothing quite like a graph or a table to convince gullible readers. This is really easy: you just make up some figures to support your argument. Nobody's ever heard of any of the "market research agencies" cited in all these business reports because the vast majority are fictitious. So fantasise about the future and ascribe it to someone who doesn't exist, "recent market research conducted by Gibduarf shows that in three years' time, almost 97% of the population still won't have a clue which one's Ant and which one's Dec."

11. The bagpipes phenomenon

But if all else fails, you can always try the ultimate manoeuvre – a career change whereby you make a virtue of something you were bad at. Be inspired by bagpipes. Bagpipes were originally invented as something which made such an awful noise that they were deployed in battle to scare away the enemy's horses. The inventions of the tank and heavy artillery somewhat undermined this functionality since horses disappeared from the battlefield, although it is tempting to think about how the tanks at Tiannamen Square might have responded to the instrumental break in "Mull of Kintyre". Anyway, undeterred by

I want a Scotland which is free
a Scotland which keeps its North Sea oil revenue
Its free universities
and its traditional bagpipe music

this technological advance, someone somewhere along the line, decided to label bagpipes as being a musical instrument, despite the fact that they continued – and continue - to emit ghastly, screeching noises. The bagpipe phenomenon – the conversion of something intrinsically awful into something admired – is the very quintessence of the Strategic Executive.

Surprisingly, however, Strategic Executives have missed out on a couple of opportunities in the realm of successful reinvention. Business literature, for example, has actually missed its niche since it really ought to supplant children's fairy tales. Fairy tales are meant to make children go to sleep but they set about this in a most bizarre way, e.g. by having a captivating story and by evoking images of all sorts of ghouls and baddies which will keep the children awake. If you really want children to fall asleep quickly, then much better a bed-time story, which begins a bit more like this….

"Once upon a time there was a company with a mission to bring about a business transformation by way of its industry leading virtualisation which would earn customer preference and recruiting and retaining world-class talent in a best-practice environment. Its management team included a Fairy Godmanager who fostered a trust-based culture amongst his team of best-in-class technology evangelists, who spearheaded….." Zzzzzzzzzzz

But at least Strategic Executives haven't got the audacity to try to make money out of their written bullshit. Unlike business book writers…

VI

DUMBING DOWN

So what makes a good book? Great plot full of unexpected but plausible twists? Interesting characters vividly described? Great literary style, packed with aphorisms, humour and perceptive insights? And how would you describe something which has none of these? Answer: a business book.

Business books are recommended by people who have never read them, namely Strategic Executives. This is because Strategic Executives never read *any* books since the act of reading suffers from a number of drawbacks including the requirement to remain quiet for extended periods of time and the inability to simultaneously talk about yourself. If Strategic Executives ever did stop to read the business books, which they recommend to the rest of us, they'd probably be mildly alarmed at some of the ideas put forward. Like performance-related pay. As opposed to bullshit-related pay.

About the author

Before looking at the contents of a book, it's important to understand the author. To extend the maxim - if those who can, do and those who can't, teach; then those who don't, won't and can't, write a business book. Business books are to literature what Gordon Brown is to smiling.

By convention a short biography of the author appears on the inside fly cover besides the obligatory flattering, touched-up photo of an all-American guy, with a Donald Trump style hairdo, exuding integrity, wisdom and gun-toting arrogance. If honesty were to prevail (something of a rarity in the business world) – this is what would be written:

Brad T Gritt III (real name something much less tough) graduated (in the Jeffrey Archer sense of the word) from Harvard with a master's degree in Incredibly Advanced Business Studies. A lazy charmer with the gift of the gab, he easily got a job as a trainee market trader for BAI bank plc. Operating in a world of über-bullshitters, he picked up many of the themes of this book as well as a series of ill-deserved bonuses. He was eventually dismissed after a botched attempt at a rogue trader fraud.

Having unsuccessfully applied for a series of unsuitably overpowered jobs, he decided to style himself as an "internet entrepreneur" whilst buying and selling cheap tat off e-bay. This abruptly stopped when he lost his BAI redundancy pay-off on purchasing what he thought was a long-lost Monet but which turned out to be a nursery schoolboy's depiction of Father Christmas.

By now totally unemployable, he turned his hand to the refuge and stock-in-trade of many a male menopause victim, freelance consultancy. Here he got a taste for cashing in on people willing to take his drivel seriously. This gave him the idea of accessing a wider circle of naïve fools by writing this book.

This book is the first that he has had published but in an effort not to appear a novice, he is holding out the titles of essays he wrote at school as previous publications.

He has a sham marriage and three children by three different women, all of whom equally revile him.

OK, perhaps I'm just jealous because I couldn't get an agency deal for this book and had to publish it myself.

The proof of the pudding - Contents

The basic truth is that business books are specious, repetitively presenting self-evident truisms as if they were something profound. For this they deploy a number of techniques, all trying to disguise the fact that the writer has nothing or very little to say. Take Larry Bossidy and Ram (sic) Charan's timeless classic, "Execution: the discipline of getting things done". The entire contents are contained in the title but somehow Mssrs Bossidy and Charan manage to prattle on for 278 pages. (Perhaps "write a business book" would be an innovative punishment to replace writing lines at school).

In writing such rubbish, there are many rules you *don't* need to abide by (like those relating to grammar and spelling, for instance) but the following rules are essential:

1. Firstly repeat what little you have to say ad nauseam. This can be done by the old introduction-body-summary structure in each and every chapter, i.e. say what you're going to say, say it, then say what you've just said. It's a bit like listening to a drunkard in a pub reflecting on the England football team's latest flop.

2. Secondly – leave a few blank pages at the end of each chapter, ostensibly for the reader to take notes but in reality just to pad the thing out a bit. An oversize font-size also has the same effect.

3. Present the bloody obvious as if it were a Eureka moment. For instance, those great business gurus Kaplan and Norton

came up with this great insight on page 319 of their 2001 masterpiece "The Strategy-Focused Organization" (note the two spelling errors in the title), "Call meetings on subjects that really matter and show up." Don't you just wish you could have come up with that idea?

4. Use of anecdotes

At school and university, students are taught that the absolute worst way to justify an argument is by anecdotal evidence. Not so for business writers, who frequently make unsubstantiated assertions backed up solely by completely unverifiable quotes. Imagine how a business book writer, regressed back to his schooldays, would cope with a typical exam question.....

> Question: Prove Pythagoras's Theorem.
>
> Answer: I recently met a CEO of the Pentagon on the 8th tee and he said, "Hey Zack, how you doing? And how's Mary-Beth: she looked mighty fine at Machine Gun Club last night. By the way, did you know that $x^2 + y^2 = z^2$ where z is the hypotenuse of a right-angled triangle and x and y are the two other sides?"

5. Invent words by adding the suffixes "-ness" or "ality" to existing words, thereby creating such ghastly monstrosities as "preparedness" and "invaluability".

6. Include ridiculously long bibliographies, comprising books with the word "how" in the titles – "How we deal with success and failure", "How to use communication to grow your business", "How to unlock your creativity", "How to make money out of writing a load of bollocks."

More sophisticated techniques for book padding

Although the above techniques are invaluable for basic rambling, the real secret to padding out a book (in addition to getting it printed on thick paper and leaving big spaces between the lines) is to deploy some real time-wasting waffle techniques. This section deals with the more sophisticated ways in which business book writers manage to spin out their work.

1. Quadrant Analysis

Quadrant Analysis basically involves dividing absolutely any decision, issue or problem (however elementary) into four scenarios, which are represented on a pseudo-academic graph divided into quarters (quadrants). Add a pretentious title and a few lines and curves which never get explained in the narrative and bingo, you have your own quadrant analysis. This totally contrived way of looking at things will produce a four-page way of saying "good morning". Here's a handy step-by-step guide.

Step 1: Setting up the Quadrants

Instead of saying that you should do A or B, it is much more sophisticated to contrive a couple of continuums and then arbitrarily divide each of them in two, thus creating the obligatory four quadrants. If this instruction strikes you as entirely random, then you have instantly grasped the essence of Quadrant Analysis.

Step 2: Fancy labels

The business book writer then needs to apply his linguistic prowess to come up with some catchy names for each of the four artificially created quadrants, complete with some spurious mathematical techniques to

add gravitas. Broadly speaking the four scenarios are always as follows:-
- Quadrant B (top right hand corner): clearly what you want to do.
- Quadrant D (bottom left): clearly what you don't want to do.
- Quadrant A (top left): action preferred by clever dicks.
- Quadrant C (bottom right): ludicrous set of circumstances resulting from applying quadrant methodology.

Step 3: The narrative

This is best illustrated by a practical example, bringing together all of the above into what would make for a great entry for Pseuds' Corner.

How to apply for a job successfully

All that need be said about job interview preparation is that interviewees should do research beforehand and need to show individuality in order to differentiate him- or herself from the multitude of other candidates. This perfectly sensible (if somewhat obvious) advice suffers from the disadvantage of only taking up three lines. Contrast this with the following gobbledegook.

Extract from Jack J Pratt III's "How to make Great Business Decisions"

Want to be a sure-fire success at getting through job interviews? All you need to remember is the Pri-dual Model, which builds on mastering the two key factors at play during job interviews:

1. Preparationednessality

2. Individuality

These 2 factors can be represented graphically with the x-axis showing the extent of preparation, so that at 10 I've researched on the internet and spoken to my business contacts at the Family Harvest Christian Fellowship, whereas at 0, I've done Jack Shite (just like the way I prepared to write this book). In short I know as much about the Corporation as an All-American Guy does about the laws of cricket.

The y-axis represents individuality with a score of 10 representing a guy who really jumps out and shouts, "I'm in-ya-face fantastic," whereas at 0, I'm just one of the sheep: you know a kind of Tony Blair in the Eye-Rack war.

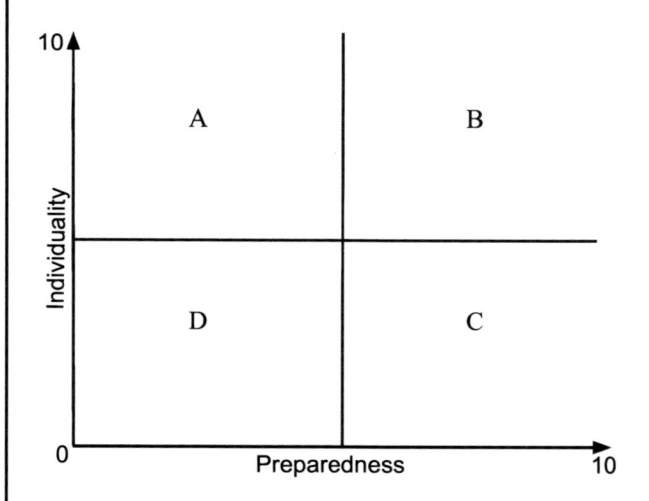

```
10↑
            |
     A      |      B
            |
            |
_____|_____
            |
            |
     D      |      C
            |
 0_____|_____→
      Preparedness      10
```

You can see what type of interviewee you are by plotting your score (on a scale of 0 to 10) for Preparednessalitous on the x-axis and Individuality (again on a scale of 0 to 10) on the y-axis. How do you find your score? Ask your friends down at the Tubby Town Mall. Or make use of my on-line Pri-dual Model tool at www.makeapratrich.com.

Once you've identified where you are, the objective is to move your position in the direction of the "Arrow of Success" in order to optimize your job application success-rate. To help with this, it's useful to divide the graph into four areas. So what type of interviewee are you?

A "Ethelred the Unready": High on individuality but low on preparednessalitousation, you're quite a distinct guy but totally ill-prepared for anything unexpected. Are you an Ethelred? Although dressing up as a parrot for the interview will get you noticed, the fact that you don't know the name of the corporation you're applying to work for (or the name of the country you're just about to invade) means you lose the job.

B "Palin" (Sarah, not Michael, by the way) – you're well prepared plus you're showing your individuality as an all-American kinda Guy. Ironclad.

C "Geek" - High on preparednessalitousationarity but low on individuality. You really suck – it's all very well swatting up on all the stats which show you can't successfully invade Middle Eastern countries, but we like someone who's gonna stand up and be counted.

D – "Quayle" (or is it spelt "Quayl"?) Low on individuality, low on kocha mocha.[1]

---

1   This is a Japanese business term which translates roughly as preparationalisationismisticness.

2. Pretentious diagrams

Notice Jack's skilful use of space-consuming graphics to further embellish his vacuous ideas. That's because diagrams are another great way of padding a book out. Regardless of how many indented bullet points, tables and italicised mumbo-jumbo the business book author's managed to cram in, written text is pretty daunting to the average reader. Especially given that the average reader of a business book is someone who's been forced to read it against his or her will. So the occasional illustration is a welcome relief. Which reminds me – must put in an irrelevant cartoon here.

RSC ADAPTS "ROMEO AND JULIET" TO A MODERN CONTEXT

Diagrams, however, are meant to be graphical representations which clarify or illustrate something which is difficult to convey in words. In business books, diagrams are designed to do the complete opposite, i.e. to convert simplistic platitudes into something apparently requiring brain-power.

The subject matter of these diagrams is often companies and for some strange reason, business book writers are (or at least were) often attracted to the example of "Fannie Mae", as the Federal National Mortgage Association in the US was known. This fascination can't be attributable to its "Carry on Innuendo" name since this is lost on writers from America, where the forenames Fannie and Randy don't provoke the schoolboy sniggering which is de rigueur in the UK.

Fannie Mae went bust when its leaders appeared to wake up one day and discover they'd lost $14.9bn. Before then, this monumental failure of a company was a natural magnet for business writers – not to point out how crap they were but the complete opposite. As an example, you can do far worse than refer to something called Fannie Mae's "Operational Excellence Strategy Map" as set out in Mssrs. Kaplan and Norton's seminal work cited above. It features 11 boxes, some of which are sub-divided into smaller boxes, all allocated across four splendid sounding layers of management-speak. Needless to say there are plenty of arrows and bullet points liberally scattered all over this smorgasbord of claptrap with such magnificent rhetoric as "Develop Culture of Accountability and Achievement", "Value-Based Partnership" and "Migrate from Pilot to Production." Strangely enough, however, nowhere does it say, "go cap in hand to US taxpayer for $370m bail-out."

3   Quality techniques

Anyone who has had any contact with a Quality Manager will know that they are past masters at padding things out. Some of them have,

THE BOARD HAVE ALL PERSONALLY TAKEN TO HEART YOUR PLEA FOR CONTINUOUS IMPROVEMENT AND WITH IMMEDIATE EFFECT ARE APPLYING THE CONCEPT TO THEIR OWN SALARIES
QUALITY MANAGER

after all, created their entire careers out of one single good idea they had in 1978. What is less widely known is that the whole phenomenon of "Quality" or "Process Improvement" specialists has sprung up from the general mayhem caused by Strategic Executives. Quality specialists constructed their discipline on the basis of being just a bit more organised than the Captain Chaos and the Cock-up Crew, who now occupy the commanding heights of the modern business world. In so doing, Quality Managers have perfected the art of making problems look so complicated and their solutions sooooo boring, that you have to wonder what motivates these guys to get up in the morning. In fact, as the chart below shows, if, first thing in the morning, Quality Managers deployed one of their numerous techniques for over-complicating things (namely decision trees), they'd never actually come to work…

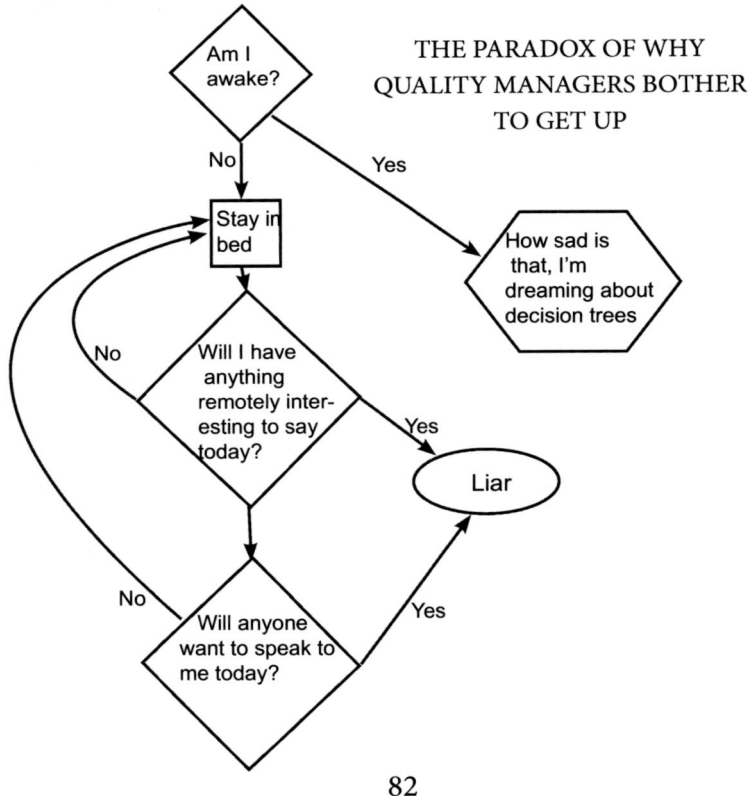

THE PARADOX OF WHY QUALITY MANAGERS BOTHER TO GET UP

- Am I awake?
  - No → Stay in bed
  - Yes → How sad is that, I'm dreaming about decision trees
- Will I have anything remotely interesting to say today?
  - No → Stay in bed
  - Yes → Liar
- Will anyone want to speak to me today?
  - No → Stay in bed
  - Yes → Liar

Needless to say business book writers have seized upon concepts such as decision trees to artificially expand their output. They've also cashed in on another Quality Manager tool for annoying the shit out of everyone - root cause analysis. This technique has elevated the childish act of repeatedly uttering the word "why" to making yourself sound like a business guru. Any tom-fool can do this – you just find a problem, ask why it has happened and whatever the response is, just say "why was that?" Keep going like this and eventually you'll get to the ultimate root cause: God.

Unfortunately not all juvenile conversational techniques are used in business which is a pity. For instance children have a wonderful tendency to state an obvious truth which is too embarrassing for adults to utter. "Mummy, why do all those people who fell asleep in the training session say it was great?"

4. Use of dialogue

One particularly annoying feature of some business books is the ghastly co-authored scenario, when the two joint authors alternate disseminating their pearls of tedium. This is hardly the Socratic dialogue at the heyday of the Greek empire: it's just they're too lazy to even bother to combine their thoughts into one coherent prose. "Ram said this, Larry said that" - or more accurately "Ram said this, Larry said this all over again."

Business book: the sequel

Can you think of any sequel which has matched the original? Some sequels were so abysmal that you didn't know they existed – "Grease 2" for example. It's almost as if the digit at the end is a measure of the awfulness of the film with, like the Richter scale, every additional number indicating something exponentially more dreadful than the previous one. "Basic Instinct 2", "Jaws 3D", "Superman IV", "Police Academy 6". And even the most avid of Sylvester Stallone fans must cringe a little at the prospect of "Rocky 12" coming out. It features the story of a centenarian making his 39th comeback to the ring and – against all odds - defeating a stereotypical representative of whatever country is alarming American public opinion at the time of filming. But at least these sequels were on the heels of a worthy original. In the case of business books, the original was worthless, so you can imagine the calibre of the follow-up.

But for the business writer, the sequel is wonderful. You get more money for trotting out the same old nonsense. And best of all you can pander to your own supreme arrogance by quoting yourself as if you were some great super-guru. "In my groundbreaking book 'Just how many boyfriends has X-factor star Mini Obscurito had?' I revealed that when she tells "Hello" magazine that she's, "finally found happiness with her new man," it actually means she's short of a few bob and is organising a whip round from the saddos who not only buy this stuff but are prepared to be seen in public with it."

Compared to the business book writer, the Strategic Executive now seems quite humble because at least he doesn't try to sell his bullshit (unless he's a management consultant). However it's not just words and letters, the Strategic Executive wades into. Oh no, the Strategic Executive takes on a wide range of academia and it's time to look at that in a bit more detail.

VII

WE DON'T NEED NO EDUCATION: THE 3Rs IN MODERN BUSINESS

A lot of what we learn at school and university is over-turned in the "real World." And it's not the long holidays, excessive drinking and appalling fashion sense because they are all alive and well at the Strategic Executive level. It's the stuff we learnt.

At university we are encouraged in free and original thinking, open debate and criticism and we are judged on the intrinsic value of our own work (our own essays, dissertations, exam answers, etc). Then we get a job and find that we all need to wear a work uniform, believe mindless mantras such as mission statements and refrain from all criticism of upper management. Above all our success is determined not by the work we do but by the "work" we are seen to be doing. Arguably some of this makes sense in that, whereas formal education is a solitary thing, a company needs to work as a team towards common goals. Other assaults on the product of our education, however, are less defensible, most noteworthy of which is the attack upon the fundamentals, the

3 Rs – reading, writing and arithmetic. In the business world it would be no understatement to say that they have been replaced by the 3 Bs – bollocks, bullshit and bastards.

1. Writing

E-mails were meant to create the paperless office. In fact they have spawned the answer-less office. But not the response-less office. Far from it. Verbal diarrhoea has given way to e-diarrhoea as Strategic Executives fall over themselves to impress their colleagues and bosses with their responses which are as vapid as they are rapid. In this section, e-mail etiquette is laid bare.

The Strategic Executive's raison d'être is to impress his boss. E-mail is an important medium for this but it suffers from one considerable drawback compared to that of speech. It doesn't have the deniability which the spoken word has. Once an e-mail is sent, it is a matter of public record of who said what, however ridiculous and offensive. This is a particular handicap for the Strategic Executive when it comes to responding to his boss's written questions, since it goes without saying that he won't know the answer to anything but the most simplistic question. Furthermore, honesty seldom pays in the Strategic Executive's world, so a truthful reply along the lines of, "I don't know, I'll try to find out", is out of the question. So what can he do?

Faced with an e-mailed question he can't answer, broadly speaking the Strategic Executive acts according to one of two scenarios.

Scenario 1: Strategic Executive knows who'll know the answer

Realistically, this scenario is the best-case for the Strategic Executive. Obviously he can't answer his boss's question himself but he knows someone who should know the answer.

I DON'T KNOW WHAT PEOPLE LIKE ME DID BEFORE BLACKBERRIES, IPADS AND EMAIL.
WORK?

In this case, the Strategic Executive can immediately impress his boss by forwarding the boss's e-mail to the "person in the know", putting the boss on copy. The Strategic Executive will usually do this immediately although sometimes he may perceive some merit in waiting a few hours for a suitably unsociable time, so that the Strategic Executive can claim additional kudos by his 24/7 working culture. The forwarded e-mail is usually accompanied by a rider something like, "That's a great question, chief. Flunkey – tell the chief how we're progressing on the "great-name-no-activity" strategic initiative."

Scenario 2: Strategic Executive clueless

More commonly, the Strategic Executive will not only not know the answer to the boss's question but also he won't know where to get it. So he sets off one of his great defining characteristics, the e-mail Jamboree, a veritable saturnalia of frantically stabbing in the electronic dark. The Jamboree (actually it's more of a car boot sale – full of tat no-one needs) comprises five basic steps.

Step 1

Firstly the Strategic Executive puts his 'phone on divert-to-voicemail in order to avoid any calls from the boss whilst his work is underway. For a Strategic Executive, this is harder than it seems since the sound of his 'phone ringing is vital to his self-esteem (it suggests someone wants or needs to talk to him). Answering his 'phone is therefore a compulsive addiction. The Strategic Executive is pathologically incapable of letting 'phone calls go through to voicemail, unless of course he identifies them as being from his wife.

Step 2

The Strategic Executive will then immediately forward the question on to his coterie of e-victims (obviously this time not putting his boss on copy since his ignorance will be exposed). Assuming the recipients include some trainee Strategic Executives then they, equally clueless, will forward the question on to a third tier. And so the e-mail Jamboree swings into action. Breeding like rabbits has got nothing on e-mailing like businessmen.

Step 3

In the absence of an immediate answer to his desperate e-mails the Strategic Executive, acutely aware that he owes a "deliverable" to his boss, then launches the second wave of the Jamboree – the chaser e-mails. This has to take place within the memory span of the Strategic Executive so can therefore be no later than two hours after the initial e-wave was launched.

This second wave is handicapped by the fact that the Strategic Executive is totally devoid of organisation skills. His in-box is more of an in-reservoir or in-ocean although it's not quite as bad as his sent items box, the contents of which bear a striking resemblance to the effluence pipe at a sewerage works.

Given this lack of organisation skills, the Strategic Executive is incapable of looking up his original e-mail and so he sends a different variant of the same question to a different first tier of victims. Not only are new people enlisted in the Jamboree but the slight variation of the question means that those who received the first question (including people who have not yet worked out what a dunce the Strategic Executive is) assume this to be a different question. This launches another wave of e-mails relating to the mutated question. One day a

Business Writer will formulate a pretentious and inaccurate formula to quantify the volume of communication generated by this process but all you really need to know is the Strategic Executive is the catalyst of an awful load of excrement.

Annoying as chaser e-mails are, they are not as infuriating as the ultimate electronic irritant, the nasty e-mail. These e-mails are sent out by a sub-genre of the type of weirdos who go on shooting sprees in American high schools. For months they secretly hoard their ammunition and then wake up one day resolving to massacre a few innocent co-workers in the office. The saving grace of this strain of weirdos is that, rather than stockpiling an arsenal of weapons of mass destruction, their arms cache comprises exclusively incriminating e-mails. The weirdo waits for his moment and then sends out something like,

> I am disappointed to note that you have failed to honour your commitment to submit your quarterly Time and Travel Analysis report in accordance with the deadline specified in my e-mail dated 5 June. This is despite my incredibly polite reminders on 29 May and 4 June. The Travel and Time Analysis report is vital to our mission-critical objectives and your failure to submit it punctually could very well trigger a tidal wave off the Norfolk coast.

Note the use of the word "disappointed" at the start. In fact they're delighted and couldn't wait to send out their poison which they've been carefully nurturing over the previous few days and weeks.

There's no in point arguing with the nasty e-mailer (he's probably got more ammunition tucked away and would love it if you put up a fight), so you have to concede. On the basis that the best form of attack is to do what your enemy least wants you to do, you have to threaten something the nasty e-mailer hates – human contact!!! So try a reply along the lines of.....

> Hi Michael
>
> Sorry about that - I'll drop by sometime soon to work out together how we can sort this out.
>
> Cheers
> Me
>
> P.S. I hope the Battle of Hastings re-enactment goes well at the weekend. Found the lucky lady on Lonelyhearts.com yet?

That'll strike terror into his heart – it exudes friendliness, the "sometime soon" means he'll be on edge constantly, the "work out together" implies collaboration, consensus and co-operation - all anathema to the nasty e-mailer.

Unfortunately the threat of human contact option is not available if the nasty e-mailer is in a different office, or even in a different country. In this case, the only viable course of action is a NATO air-strike: there are too many humans on the planet for its own good and we can easily do without the nasty e-mailers.

But let's not malign e-mails with talk of the nasty e-mailer because e-mails are a medium for great humour in the workplace. There's the old "send an e-mail to someone with a similar name to the intended recipient" routine. Or the "blurt out a response to the first line of an e-mail without reading the rest of it" pitfall.

And then there are the "Reply to all" by mistake e-mails. Take the Communications Director's announcement of a meeting to launch the annual major restructuring of the marketing department. To the uninitiated this list of new roles might appear like the results to the Silly Job Titles Competition. In fact it is a communiqué which has been the subject of considerable thought (much more than the restructuring itself) so you can't help but feel a little sympathy when the only reply it elicits is from Joan in Accounts who tells the whole World that she won't be able to attend the meeting because her son Jack's constipated.

Anyway – back to the e-mail Jamboree.

Step 4

In the way that a only a single sperm out of billions achieves its goal then sooner or later the Jamboree ends up with the question coming to someone who knows the answer.

For the Strategic Executive this is a highly dangerous moment since his objective is to impress his boss but so many people are now involved that there is a real danger that the answer will find its way back to the boss without the Strategic Executive getting the credit or, worse still, without him even knowing that the boss has received his answer. At this point the Strategic Executive reverses his tactic – instead of widening the communication channel, it is now essential that he closes it down. Ideally he'll be able to 'phone the person with the answer so that he can get it verbally and exclusively. This will leave the field clear for the Strategic Executive to be the first person to write down the answer. He can then pretend he knew the answer all along or worked it out for himself and all the other e-mails were ways of just keeping his colleagues on their toes.

Step 5

The problem for the Strategic Executive is that, although he has *found* the answer, in light of his grotesque ignorance of business, he won't actually *understand* it. Time for waffle - what Jack the Ripper was to surgery, the Strategic Executive is to succinct answers. The Strategic Executive then emits an e-mail which reads like a mixture of crossword clues and the lyrics to "A whiter shade of pale". However he knows that if he puts in enough jargon, repetition and general bluster, the answer will be in there somewhere and hopes his boss will either work it out or be too embarrassed to admit that he can't.

2. Reading

One of the key weapons (a veritable kalashnikov in fact) in the Strategic Executive's armoury is "skim reading", the mythical practice of absorbing the contents of a book without actually reading it. Outside the business world, you'd call it flicking through a book, looking at the pictures. The Strategic Executive has, however, elevated this symptom of his Attention Deficit Hyperactivity Disorder approach to work to an art that only people with their photographic memories can undertake. The absurdity of this technique is best illustrated by describing some of its sister concepts:

Skim driving – the practice of only paying attention to 1 in 3 road signs and thereby disregarding Road Traffic Act niceties like giving way to fellow road-users and believing that inconvenient parking restrictions can be circumvented by putting your hazard lights on.

Skim adding – the art of selectively adding only a few of the numbers in a column with a nice sub-total at the bottom. Most commonly used by bankers when assessing credit worthiness of a trailer-park trash mortgage request.

Skim working – something Strategic Executives do. Also known as working from home.

There are two defences of skim reading. Firstly, it doesn't suffer from one disadvantage of thorough, word-for-word, literal reading where every word needs to be taken as gospel. Consider the poor Jehovah's witnesses – because there's not a single word in the Bible showing Jesus celebrating his birthday, not only do they not celebrate their own birthdays but they give Christmas a miss as well. The author cannot claim to have read the Bible cover to cover but to the best of my knowledge, there's also no record of Jesus having a dump but that doesn't mean we should all strive for perpetual constipation.

Secondly, let's be honest, who can blame anyone from trying to avoid reading all the crap that the business world produces? Business literature is a huge deterrent to reading.

One component of this deterrent is the vocabulary used in business "literature". Much as people might complain about how "political correctness" has driven many day-to-day words from the English language, the real culprit is "HR correctness". Basic words such as "problem" and "weakness" are being hounded out of existence by nebulous euphemisms like "challenging opportunity" and "area for development". A by-product of this is that the training "facilitators" (another ridiculous word) will never criticise or make negative remarks about the trainees or participants. This makes for exceeding tedium because, let's face it, we all like nothing more than laughing at other people's failings.

One word above all has achieved a sickening pre-eminence – "proactive." It is now worthless to be seen to be reactive – however quick – to the world around us; much better to be seen as some obnoxious know-all, "proactively" spouting mumbo-jumbo based on no greater foundation than an over-fertilised imagination. A compensating feature of "proactive" people is that they are actually "no-active", i.e. for all their talk, they don't actually *do* anything.

3. Arithmetic

If Strategic Executives are barely literate, then they are completely innumerate. A table or graph strikes them with horror, as does anybody who gets involved with numbers, in particular accountants, tax men and people who like cricket.

It is obvious that Strategic Executives have a problem with numbers because they will use words such as "many", "numerous" and "several" when they word they are looking for is "one." Their natural insecurity (or is it an awareness of their own fakeness?) means that, when challenged, they are programmed never to say, "there is just one reason for this." Instead they list out reasons, which turn out to be one reason

GOLDEN RULE FOR STRATEGIC EXECUTIVES: NEVER GIVE A STRAIGHT ANSWER TO A QUESTION INVOLVING NUMBERS

"I have some close contacts in the city who would say that that's difficult to call in the present economic climate, but you're looking at a figure anywhere between 0 and 1.3 trillion."

"I only asked you which floor?"

restated several different ways, petering out with the words, "etcetera, etcetera." Or "blah blah blah." They compound the buffoonery by prefixing the explanations with "firstly", "secondly" and very rapidly losing count, so the word "thirdly" is never heard in a business context.

Numerate people will very quickly realise this deficiency and can readily exploit it by inventing statistics to suit their arguments. Thus there are a number of statistical tricks to fool a Strategic Executive. For example, consider the following sequence.

Year	Sales (£m)
2007	830
2008	950
2009	1100
2010	1250
2011	1400
2012	1540
2013	1660

Sales have clearly grown, having doubled over the six years in question. But let's say we want the Strategic Executive to think the opposite - let's introduce percentage growth.

Year	Sales growth %
2007	N/A
2008	14%
2009	16%
2010	14%
2011	12%
2012	10%
2013	8%

That's better – the sales growth doesn't look so impressive now. And finally, the masterstroke – sales growth percentage compared to the previous year.

Year	Sales growth % compared to prior year
2007	N/A
2008	N/A
2009	+2%
2010	-2%
2011	-2%
2012	-2%
2013	-2%

Bingo! What a miserable story of long-term decline.

And we didn't even resort to the old familiar tactic of excluding "one-offs." Every period is full of one-offs so it's ridiculous to exclude selected ones, unless of course you're desperate to present black as white. To illustrate the point, if we exclude one-offs, all of the following statements are true.

Britain has never had a woman Prime Minister.
1966 was an uneventful year for the England football team.
The Titanic had an impeccable safety record.

In addition to the old "excluding one-offs" line, the number manipulator (I think the word I'm looking for is accountant) has a whole gallery of random-number generator formulae and tricks which can produce whatever results he wants. The words he uses in this context are things like net present value, seasonal adjustments and foreign exchange movements but, for all the sense it makes, he might as well say, "abracadabra".

So, armed with his literacy and numeracy skills, the Strategic Executive draws upon all his talents to mastermind his ultimate creation, the PowerPoint presentation.

VIII

WAKE UP CALL - THE LIFE AND TIMES OF POWERPOINT

AFTER A BRIEF DISCUSION, THE ELDERS OF THE NBOTO-MKOKO TRIBE CONCLUDED THAT, AS SADISTIC RITUALS GO, POWERPOINT WOULD BE A WORTHY REPLACEMENT TO THEIR TRADITIONAL CANNIBALISM

Powerpoint: the early years

The origins of Powerpoint are the subject of some academic debate. Not much, but some. And here it is, in its entirety.

For centuries orators relied upon what they had to say and the way they said it in order to captivate and retain their audience's attention. People who had nothing to say, said nothing. And then the monstrous 20th century dawned – two World Wars, the invention of weapons of mass destruction and the advent of Alan Carr, Chatty Man. As yet we don't know how history books will label the second half of the twentieth century in the UK. We know that the first half comprised the Edwardian era, the inter-war years and a couple of "during the war" periods. But what about the second half? It can't be called the Elizabethan era since we've had one of them already, so there is a need for a name which captures the zeitgeist of the last few decades. Celebrities, gossip magazines and 'Britain's Got Talent". Here are a few suggestions.

Just as there was the Great Depression, we've now had the Great Dumb-down. There's already been a Renaissance so what about a Denaissance? Whatever it is, it's the complete opposite of an Enlightenment, so how about the Encrapment Era?

And just as inventions such as Caxton's printing press and Stephenson's Rocket came to be pivotal reference points of their periods, so will Fish's PowerPoint come to be emblematic of the late 20th century. Why *Fish's* Powerpoint? Fair question because it completely understates the role of Jade Goody. So here's the full story.

Michael Fish's association with PowerPoint is derived from the fact that weathermen in the 1980s were amongst the early pioneers of people who stood in front of a changing animated screen whilst spouting nonsense. In his case – wildly inaccurate weather forecasts. Their

THERE IS EVIDENCE THAT THE ORIGINS OF POWERPOINT CAN BE TRACED BACK TO PREHISTORIC TIMES

pretentious claims to infallibility in the face of demonstrable evidence to the contrary was a natural fit with the modern Strategic Executive. The problem with the weather forecast, however, was that it was all too brief and had some sort of intellectual foundation, so the inventors of PowerPoint needed to look elsewhere for duration, tedium and sheer stupidity. And that's where Jade Goody came in. "Big Brother live" proved that something could be made of long, soporific material featuring stupid people. Jade Goody was its greatest star. What a legacy - totally devoid of talent, she achieved fame for being coarse and imbecilic.

There were of course other contributory factors to the rise of PowerPoint – the US Bush Government's "war on punctuation" led to the invention of the bullet point. And then God (or more precisely Bill Gates) created PowerPoint and the lunatics have been taking over the asylum ever since.

PowerPoint is now unstoppable. Suddenly those pre-PowerPoint days when the acetates kept jamming up the photocopier are distant, fond memories. History provides some comfort in that there have been several seminal moments when there have been book-burning exercises, such as the Bonfire of Vanities or whatever the name is for the bit when Henry VIII got in a strop with the Church for not letting him marry Anne Boleyn. Wouldn't it be wonderful if some such equivalent for PowerPoint presentations were introduced? Everyone could assemble around a big screen and a horrible virus or worm would be introduced which – before our eyes - would systematically eat away at all those bullet points, logos and corny slogans.

But we're stuck with it, so it's better to learn how to play the PowerPoint game. Being able to prepare a PowerPoint presentation is an essential tool in the modern Strategic Executive's armoury. It is also an undoubted art form. The good news is the presentation need not be interesting, have a structure or contain anything of remote insight or value. The bad news is that it has to be extremely and unnecessarily long. Basically, although completely pointless, the presentation needs to have lots of point in it.

Why is PowerPoint so boring?

Expectations play a vital role in determining how boring something seems. For example, the England football team and British women tennis players are both mediocre and never get further than the last 16. However since we expect one lot to beat the world and the other to beat a hasty retreat, our views of their performance levels are wildly different.

In light of this, it is remarkable that Strategic Executives continue to bore the socks off everyone. The audience's expectations are rock bottom to start with (not dissimilar to that sinking feeling you get when the battery on the remote control runs out just as the opening credits of "Songs of Praise" start to roll). And yet somehow they manage to disappoint. How do they do it?

A few basic rules

The Strategic Executive's over-riding objective of any PowerPoint presentation is to avoid being asked any questions during or at the end of the presentation. Questions could expose his superficial knowledge of the subject matter, even though he is holding himself out as a world expert. To head off this risk, there are three elements to the compilation and delivery of a really effective lullaby.

1. Theatrical introduction

Time wasting is an important component of avoiding questions: the more time the Strategic Executive's presentation takes, the less time for questions and even less time for "answers". There are a few theatrics that the Strategic Executive can resort to.

- Firstly he will fritter away a few crucial moments right at the start by pretending there's a technological hitch, e.g. with the microphone or the remote control. Then he will impress his audience with his ability to repair it with the trusted "give it a blow and a tap" routine. Double whammy – time wasted, audience impressed.

- If you're talking to a new audience, then a word of self-introduction will not go amiss. But a whole dissertation will. If, however, your audience does already know you, then they'll also already know what a tosspot you are, so it's best not to dwell on this area for too long.

- Fairly early on in the presentation, the Strategic Executive will come out with the old, "let's do a little survey" routine. He'll ask for a show of hands to prove a point that he hasn't yet made. Of course nine times out of ten, he doesn't get the result he wants, although to be fair, usually about 85% of people don't put their hand up at all (since voting in your sleep is not easy). The Strategic Executive can then flatter his audience with some sort of line about what an unrepresentatively sophisticated audience they are, before carrying on regardless with his original point.

2. Presentational style

Everyone knows that the basic rule of a PowerPoint presentation is to stand still and deliver in a monotone but there are other tricks of the trade if you really want to have them gagging for you to stop.

- Start your presentation with a joke but deliver it in such a lame way that nobody laughs. Any joke will do, so you can choose one that is genuinely funny. The challenge then is to link it to rest of your presentation which is neither genuine nor funny. Anyway once The Joke is out of the way, the audience will know that the only half-decent line in the presentation is history, so they can safely let their minds wander onto more interesting things, like speculating on what you're like in bed. So, in order to subliminally influence them into giving you a good score in this respect, you can deploy one or more of the numerous suggestive terms used in business-speak, e.g. customer intimacy, getting into bed with a strategic partner, market penetration, etc.

- Not long after your lame joke, it's imperative to utter the, "I'm not here to plug the work of BAI plc," line. What are you then? A charity worker? It's just another example of business-speak meaning the complete opposite of what the words say. Like the much hallowed expression, "with all due respect," which is the inevitable preamble to a below-the-belt insult.

- Elimination of the possibility of questions during the presentation is easy: just say that you'll only take questions at the end. Don't say that it's because you know sod-all about what you're talking about, but that it's, "in the interests of time management." You then have free rein over the entire course of the presentation to deploy to full advantage your questions-avoidance strategy.

- When presenting, make sure to frequently say "of course" and "obviously" when you are about to same something unknown, esoteric or, more commonly, completely made-up. Those of the audience still conscious may thereby take the view that if such esoteric facts are obvious to you, then you must be very learned and/or they themselves must be very stupid.

- Make sure at some stage in the presentation, you accidentally skip on too quickly to the next slide and have to jump back a slide. This operation should be completely mishandled in such a way that you end up having to scroll through the entire presentation to find out where you're meant to be. This is real torture for the audience since they think they've made progress only to be dragged back into one of your tedious tables or daft graphs which they thought they'd seen the last of. In so doing, you can also reveal the number of slides in your presentation. It's a sure-fire way to completely demoralise them - just when they thought you were wrapping up, they find that you've only edged your way to slide 33 of 152.

3. Content

Of course, however poor your presentational style and however many time wasting techniques you've deployed en route, the aim to avoid questions at all costs will be completely torpedoed if the content of your presentation is in any way interesting, informative or entertaining. Content is vital: when preparing your slides, think terms and conditions of a hire purchase agreement.

- Clutter as much business-speak as possible on to all slides. This way, there's bound to be something which can address any question you might receive. Remember that most studies on the subject say that audiences retain at most only three to five facts from a presentation so it is important that your presentation contains at least 5,000. The three things they will remember are listed below and as you can see, none of them is particularly conducive to asking a question.
  a) You are boring;
  b) You are so boring; and
  c) You are so Party Political Broadcast.

- Don't worry about structure: in fact it helps if the presentation is rambling and incoherent, since this will very quickly divert your audience from what you are talking about. The ultimate accolade is that they may come to the conclusion that you know so much about your subject matter that it's proved impossible to structure it in an organised way. Alternatively you can always follow the example of many Strategic Executives and present so abysmally that the audience starts to believe you are in the early stages of Altzeimer's. If you can get your audience in this zone, it's a good place to be because not only will they not ask questions but, out of sheer pity, they'll become remarkably generous in their applause.

- Use as many acronyms as possible and only explain about 28% of them. This again will make you look authoritative on your subject matter and further deter questions.

- Use graphs to complicate the bleeding obvious but avoid the use of tables since these include numbers which are the nemesis of Strategic Executives.

- In the unlikely event that you have something interesting or revelatory to say, make sure you tuck it away into an obscure section and deliver the news in such a deadpan manner that nobody notices.

The proof of the pudding

And so we come towards the highlight of the presentation, the end. The moment of truth. Have you been successful in bullshitting off the possibility of any question which might expose you as the fake you are? There are a few final actions you can take to minimise the possibility of questions.

- The best way to get a laugh at the end of your presentation is to say something like, "thank you for listening: I see we've lasted a bit longer than scheduled and I'm sure you've all got much more important things to do than listen to me talk about my great passion." This sentence is one of the few heartfelt things a Strategic Executive ever says, or at least it would be if the word "listening" were substituted by "not snoring." Anyway it always gets a laugh, not due to its intrinsic wit but as the kind of laugh you hear when a naughty schoolboy realises that he's got away with misbehaving in class. However since all those asleep will not realise that everyone else was in a similar state, they'll assume that you've entertained your audience throughout your spiel.

- It is now customary to end a presentation with a slide with the sole word "Questions?" This is the great bluff of the Strategic

Executive. Make it look like you really want them to ask a question even though you're shitting bricks at the prospect.

Don't forget that the odds are stacked in your favour at this stage – few attendees will want to prolong the agony of hearing you talk. Even fewer will be convinced that they were awake throughout the entire presentation and can therefore be 100% sure that any question they have in mind hasn't already been dealt with. If you see the dreaded hand going up (in the manner of the cricket umpire just about to uphold an LBW appeal), try not to respond by saying, "oh shit." All is not lost. Instead, it's important to compliment the questioner on his question and then deploy one of a variety of responses, none of which even attempt to answer the question. For example:-

"That's an area I'm particularly interested in but regrettably I didn't have the time to do it justice today but I will be dealing with that very point in another series of presentations later this year."
"Brian's going to talk a bit about that later on in his session on, 'Disaster Recovery Plans: who gives a damn?'"
"Oh goodness me, is that the time? I'm already late for a meeting with the President of the Galaxy."

Follow up

It's important to carry on the façade of being interesting long after everyone's seen you for the crushing bore you are, so here are a few essential follow-up actions.

- Make sure you circulate your presentation afterwards. Nobody would dream of looking at it but it gives the appearance of being useful.

- Provide decent food: that way the audience will enjoy at least something that day and they may confuse their enjoyment of the food with the experience of your presentation. A common pitfall is to provide nice food but not enopugh of it. Don't forget that the average ratio of chins to people in a PowerPoint presentation audience is 4:1 so these tubbies know how to scoff their way through canapés, vol-au-vents, salmon sandwiches and the like.

The future of PowerPoint

So will it ever end? Can it get any worse? PowerPoint's hegemony is such that it is difficult to see where it will stop. It may go the route of many cultural icons and become the subject matter of a degree in its own right.

Alternatively could PowerPoint expand into television? Nowadays murder-mystery dramas have moved crimes away from being solved by conventional detective work to being fathomed out by people writing on glass walls in dark rooms and specialising in things like criminal psychology or forensic science. Perhaps one day, a new maverick cop, with a troubled personal life, will explode on the scene. He'll solve crimes by microscopically analysing the PowerPoint presentations which the murderers conveniently (but rather implausibly) leave behind at the murder scene.

And it can only be question of time before a new perfume is launched....

PowerPoint, Eau de bullshit
For the man who doesn't need to know

But it is in the Battle of the Sexes that the advance of PowerPoint is likely to have its most dramatic effects. At the moment it is overwhelmingly men who use PowerPoint to cover for the fact that they haven't done or can't do any work. But sexual emancipation is inevitable and before too long, women will take advantage of it on a similar scale. This will have bizarre consequences in that they will actually abandon the work place and return to their "traditional" housewife role to take their revenge. The Strategic Executive will arrive home to find on the Dining Room table a 36" plasma screen with a slide entitled "Culinary excellence" and a wife who'll explain that "we at 54 Bosworth Street are passionate about our mission to create an unparalleled cuisinalistic experience. We have a vision of culinary excellence – unfortunately at the moment it is just a vision, so piss off down to Pizza Hut if you want some food right now."

So now we've analysed PowerPoint, it's time to look at its habitat.

IX

THE COURT OF KING CARACTACUS

In centuries gone by, the great and good (or at least the rich) of the kingdom would dress up and gather at the King's palace. They would eat piles of unnecessarily decorated food and participate in nonsensical time-wasting ceremonies involving rods, robes and ribbons. Virtually nothing was achieved but everybody felt very important. Nowadays this basic human need of the overpaid is fulfilled by business conferences. Except that in the 21st Century the snivelling courtiers aren't foreign princes and noble lords: they are modern businessmen. Strategic Executives who like nothing more than spending their time prancing about, eating, boasting and, above all, doing as little work as possible.

However it is not easy to spend lots of money and waste lots of time, whilst appearing to be doing something sensible and extremely important. So, to get away with this, the conference organisers and the Strategic Executive attendees need to enter into a great charade to make it appear that they are doing something worthwhile. The first trick is to come up with a decent title for the conference. So, rather than being honest and billing it as "a series of boring presentations", it's best to come up with an enticing and pretentious title featuring the occasional made-up word. Something like, "Cloudism: the new paradigm for the new millennium and beyond." Any connection to the underlying content is, of course, entirely coincidental.

A second trick is to reinvent your identity for the day: conference attendees are curiously – and entirely incorrectly – known as delegates. The technical definition of a delegate is somebody elected by their peers to represent and articulate the latters' views. Attendees at conferences are, by contrast, *reviled* by their peers and their utterances represent nothing more than their own (half-baked and ignorant) prejudices. Nobody voted for them to attend the conference so a more technically accurate description would be "volunteer" although of course the most appropriate term to be applied would be "tosspot."

Upon arrival at the conference, tosspots receive a "delegate's pack". This comprises a redundant note-pad (Strategic Executives never take notes since to do so would be to recognise that somebody knows something they didn't), an even more redundant map of how to get there (bearing in mind they've already arrived) and the agenda for the day's crap. This is all accompanied by a few flyers, so-called because they are designed to drop out of the pack upon opening. All in all about as useful as a helicopter ejector seat. Or Eric Pickles.

Armed with their delegate packs and having had a cup of coffee and ignored the piles of croissants and Danish pastries (they were looking for a full English), the delegates enter the conference hall for their first exposure to the Master of Ceremonies, the star of the day, the conference chairman.

King for the day

Wouldn't it be great if, for 24 hours only, there would be a Pinnochio nose day when, like the Disney character, we all woke up and found that the sizes of our noses reflected the number of lies we had told in our lives? No doubt a number of prominent politicians would not be making many public appearances that day but, more startlingly, conference chairmen across the land would awake to find their proboscises resembled the Severn bridge.

This is because the conference chairman's job is to tell lies all day, faithfully acting in his capacity of cheer-leader for the presentations, however vacuous, misleading or soporific. Therefore virtually all of his utterances are porkies, favourites amongst which being:

"Thank you for that fascinating insight into...."
"And now we're going to hear from a leading and world-renowned expert on...."

"Having spoken to a number of you during the lunch-break….."
"I'm sure I speak for us all when I say that we can't wait for next year's conference."

It is traditional that the chairman starts the proceedings by informing his audience of the location of the fire exits. This is not in anticipation of a sudden stampede to get out, brought about by a Eureka moment amongst the delegates of what tedium they are about to endure, but by Health & Safety regulations. How curious that of all the laws chosen to be read out to a large number of businessmen, the one they elect for is Health & Safety. Nothing about insider dealing, misappropriation of public funds or fraudulent expense claims - just the exit strategy, if something goes horribly wrong. Perhaps not so strange, after all.

Some brave chairmen will also ask the delegates to switch off their mobile phones but since this is tantamount to asking them to commit suicide, this request is now dying out.

Legal requirements out of the way and, having read some idiot's guide on chairmanship, the chairman will then crack a politically incorrect joke (which will turn out to be the only moment of humour in the entire day) before embarking upon his introduction to the day's first advert, sorry I meant "presentation." The first self-publicist is often referred to as the "Guest of Honour" – the honour being that he gets to leave the conference before anyone else, i.e. immediately after his own speech.

The Courtiers

Mentally exhausted by the strain of having had to keep quiet for anything up to 90 minutes, the delegates adjourn for their mid-morning coffee break. This provides the delegates with their first real opportunity to mingle amongst fellow Strategic Executives and impress them with their business bullshit. Conference delegates broadly speaking fall into the following eight categories and these can be readily discerned at this stage.

1. On-the-pull

Almost exclusively found at conferences with overnight stays, these characters have only volunteered because they perceive an opportunity of shagging at the company's expense. They therefore have zero interest in the conference material but do have the redeeming feature that, as a consequence, they treat the conference material and attendees with the contempt they deserve (unless she's got long legs and big tits).

2   Freelance consultant

These guys proliferate at conferences. They are typically men in mid-life crisis ousted from a proper job by younger, keener and better staff and now frittering away their redundancy pay under the delusion that they can make a neat buck from companies out there who would pay to hear their pet theories and business models. For them, the coffee break is the highlight of the day since they operate under the sad misapprehension that during this time, they will stumble across a CEO who is gagging to appoint someone to advise on their obscure specialism.

The tragic reality about a mid-life crisis is that you have to grin and bear it. Or write a book taking the piss out of it.

3   Business fundamentalists

Astonishingly business conferences are frequented by a contingent of people who actually take the proceedings at face value. Gullible, impressionable and vulnerable - in other societies, these people might become suicide bombers, members of the Church of Scientology or West Ham United football fans but in the corporate world they have been radicalised into believing that the extremist propaganda of Strategic Executives is for real.

4   Unemployable

Despatched to the conference by their employers as part of their "training and development plan" or some sort of Soviet Union style "Corrective Action Plan", these characters are readily identifiable by the fact that they are a sandwich short of a picnic or, in conference parlance, a slide short of a presentation.

5   Axe-grinder

These characters have been attracted to the conference because they believe that it will afford them several opportunities to make their one and only clever-dick business theory or observation over and over again. They skew all conversations to that one point, intervene at the Q&A session and even manage to bore the taxi-driver on the way home. There's an outside chance you might be in the presence of a modern-day Copernicus, centuries ahead of his time. More likely, he's Norman Nomates to be avoided like the plague.

6   The "I haven't a clue why I'm here" brigade. Sponsored by Simon Hughes.

7   Too senior to be polite

Occasionally there are delegates who are genuinely important decision-makers. They may be guest speakers. These people are instantly recognisable by their thoroughly obnoxious behaviour and complete inability to do anything for themselves. They make no attempt to mingle, grunt when introduced to people and only spring to life when they realise they have a conversational opportunity to brag about how successful and rich they are or to tell some exaggerated anecdote in which they have a starring role as a no-nonsense, tell-'em as it is, cure-all Superman.

8   Platinum Sponsors

Mugs who paid an inflated price to get their crappy display stand stuck up in a far-flung corner of the exhibition hall.

Luncheon

An important part of the conference is the "networking sessions" (as extended lunch-break buffets have now been rebranded) where Strategic Executives – armed with drink, food and BlackBerry – intermingle. In so doing they have to confront the businessman's perennial challenge: how to eat from a paper plate and drink from a plastic glass whilst simultaneously standing up and talking bullshit. This can, of course, go horribly wrong and many a trainee Strategic Executive has spat over his interlocutor, spilt his drink or dropped a devil's horseback on the floor and then stamped it nicely into the Paisley carpet whilst shifting his weight from foot to foot, desperately waiting for his opportunity to butt into the conversation with one of his self-aggrandising anecdotes.

Conference catering staff take their revenge on all the pomposity and wastefulness of the day by laying out buffets of food which are entirely unsuitable for this mode of eating. There are vol-au-vents deliberately designed to be fractionally too big to put in your mouth in one go, sandwiches where the fillings squirt out as soon as they are bitten into and chicken pieces coated in superglue. The waitresses then exacerbate the ordeal by persistently interrupting your witty repartee to offer your audience their 18th mini quiche lorraine but then being nowhere to be seen when you have four used cocktail sticks to dispose of.

Battling away in these adverse conditions, the Strategic Executives need to adhere to the handful of essential components to conference conversations – first amongst these is asking a question and then looking around the room to see if there's anyone more interesting to talk to. Another real pièce de resistance for conference conversation is name-dropping.

Name-dropping is a key component of puffing up your image. Once you recognise someone (or better still a group of someones) who is likely to be impressed by comments such as "I once met Lord Such-and-Saatchi" or "I was a confidant of Sir So-and-So", it is imperative to home in on them and hold court. Whilst experienced Strategic Executives will know that it is paramount to pretend to have heard of every company or person that a fellow delegate mentions, the nightmare scenario for the name-dropper is to find himself with less star-struck (some might say "honest") attendees and eliciting responses along the lines of, "never heard of him", "who?" or, "not that arsehole."

The Afternoon Pageants

Tanked up with sparkling water and those disgusting little boiled sweets which can only be found in conferences, one of the main challenges in the afternoon is to avoid drawing attention to oneself by conspicuous and sustained farting. Experienced conference-goers have developed such techniques as letting them out quietly, covering them up with a loud cough or waiting for a round of applause. None of these tactics of course disguises the smell but various techniques meticulously honed as a schoolboy (such as staring at your neighbour with a mildly disgusted air) can be put to good effect once again.

The main challenge of the afternoon, however, is not flatulence but somnia. The human body is designed to take a siesta in the early to mid afternoon and conference organisers know this by deploying their most extreme snore inducers as presenters in the graveyard slot which is the afternoon session. By 2.45 p.m., most conferences resemble the Annual General Meeting of Narcoleptics Anonymous. It is easy to generalise, however, and miss the fact that there are several forms of Conference-snoozing, of varying comedic value. Delegates can try to stay awake by spotting into which category their colleagues are falling (asleep).

Type of sleep	Description	Sleeper's tactics on waking up
Nod off	The most common form of conference dozing– after about 10 to 15 minutes of resistance. The victim gradually adopts the traditional chin-down position. Can last for anything up to one hour although often punctuated by fleeting awakenings brought about by the mention of words resembling the dozer's name.	The great advantage of the nod-off position is that it resembles the posture adopted by someone surreptitiously working on their BlackBerry. Therefore upon reawakening, it is important to conspicuously brandish the said BlackBerry, accompanied by your best "I've just received an incredibly important e-mail" face. As a last resort the old, "I was resting my eyelids" line can be deployed.

Type of sleep	Description	Sleeper's tactics on waking up
Grunt-snore	The Nod-off position can very quickly escalate into a Grunt-snore, unique to conferences, cinemas and snooker matches. These are not the rhythmic near-purring of traditional snoring so much as an abrupt, almost indignant, honk suddenly emitted at high volume and often accompanied by a violent jolt.	Often the Grunt-snore itself is the cause of the victim's reawakening. It is important that the Grunt-snore is immediately disguised as a bad cough so, upon re-awakening, the victim should emit a series of subtly changing coughs, the first resembling the Grunt-snore, the latter ones closer to a conventional cough.
Full Slump	Slouched forward, head resting on hands and arms, the *Full Slump* is the most appropriate reaction to the tedious drivel imposed during conferences.	It is very difficult to cover up the Full Slump (especially if accompanied by Grunt-snores). Best hope is that everyone else was asleep and the presenter couldn't care less as long as he still gets paid.

The Jousting

Sooner or later – in order to pad out the day a bit – the chairman will open the floor for the Q&A (questions and "answers") session. By convention nobody wants to ask the first question, so there is always a pregnant pause, until one of the planted questioners pipes up with his anodyne question prefaced by an oleaginous comment such as, "Thank you to the panel for that incisive and thought-provoking overview."

Once this little ritual is out of the way, real questions commence but more often than not turn out to be mini-speeches, ending with the words, "Does the panel agree with that?" This conclusion makes the optimistic assumption that the Panel was listening.

An essential part of the Q&A ritual is pretty Marketing Assistants (girls who dropped out in the third week of their Media studies course at the University of Little Backwater) rushing to the questioners armed with microphones which – despite the existence of the huge technical station located in the middle of the conference room impinging upon the view of 45% of the audience – have only two volume settings: far too loud and inaudible. It is traditional that the microphone is given to the questioner half-way through his question and that the recipient's knee-jerk instinct is to check it's turned on. Why they do this is a mystery. It's a bit like stepping on a bus and asking the driver if the key is in the ignition.

Once the question is posed, the chairman then engages in the time-honoured practice of allocating the question to the wrong panellist who, following the business mantra of never admitting that you know sweet FA about the matter under discussion, follows the equally ancient practice of "answering" the question with a load of bollocks. Realising that a question about David Cameron's policy on schools is being answered with observations on Cameron Diaz's choice of shoes, the chairman – adding to the size of his Pinnochio nose - will rescue the situation by playing the "I want to fit in as many questions as possible so let's move on to another question" card.

At least a Q&A session vaguely does what it says on the packet. OK, the "A" should really stand for "avoidance", rather than "answers" but at least the Q is a fair descriptor, so "Q&A" goes at least 50% of the way towards describing what's going on. The same cannot be said of the other famous acronym in which the letter "Q" appears, namely the

FAQ, so-called "frequently asked questions". FAQ is one of the great misnomers of the business world. FAQs are in fact inconceivable and never asked questions. If you google "FAQ", after the inevitable link to the Wikipedia definition, the first website you are directed to commences with the following question which can thus lay claim to being the most frequently asked question in the World:

"What are the benefits of posting peer-reviewed papers to PubMed Central?"

On the next link, you will learn that a "frequently asked question" concerning the 2011 census was, "What if I'm in a residential home on census day?" Answer, "You're Bruce Forsyth."

Even tax advisers will be surprised to learn that the 7th most frequently asked question about their subject matter is, "What is the American Recovery and Reinvestment Act of 2009?"

Closing ceremony

Conferences always finish early so the chairman will implore attendees to use the saved time by completing the evaluation survey and most attendees, experiencing a feeling of gratitude for the early finish and guilt for their inattention over the previous six hours, give maximum marks to all questions. The questions are entirely predictable concentrating on the conference material and quality of the presentations. Thus the opportunity to undertake some really interesting research goes begging. Imagine what a great body of anthropological and social historical data would be constructed over time, if the questions were along the lines of:-

- How much time did you spend asleep today?
- Do you recall anything remotely interesting?
- How many farts did you emit during the afternoon session?
- On a scale of 1 to 10, how much of a prat are you?
- How many chins have you got?

In pure theory, delegates return from a conference and follow up the contacts they have made, introduce ideas they have learnt and refer leads and opportunities to their colleagues. In pure practice, however, all that happens is that delegates carry on as before except that they now receive nauseating and repetitive e-mails from the conference organisers boasting about what a great day it was and encouraging the participants to attend a thinly disguised re-run under another title. Which, of course, the Strategic Executives, in their never-ending quest to mismanage their time, are more than happy to do.

So let's move away from our trusty friend the Strategic Executive (don't worry we haven't finished with him) and turn to people even more unpopular.

X

THE ROOT OF ALL EVIL

It's all too easy to poke fun at economists. So here goes.

In their wibbly-wobbly, wishy-washy, topsy-turvy world, the economist is basically a sort of witch doctor, who, like Dusty Bin, can come up with a variety of answers to the same question, based on gobbledegook which nobody understands and nobody dares question.

So basically when a chief economist of something-in-the-City pops up to explain a random statistic which the BBC is making a fuss of on a no-news day, they might as well say, "let's go live to lottery HQ where Guinevere is about to tell us what's going to happen to interest rates." And when BBC News' Hugh Edwards says, "we're now going to hear from our economics editor Stephanie Flanders," you then see her launch into her predictions for the deliberations of the Bank of England monetary policy committee. What you don't see is her off-air preparation routine. She dons an extravagant head-dress made of bamboo, straw and flowers, throws a few bones on the table and does a charming little rain-dance. "Inflation expected to fall," the tea leaves say.

> I really do feel that if we say that our prediction about the world ending next month after an invasion by 4-headed Martian Yettis, has been endorsed by leading economists, it'll be totally discredited.

Convinced? OK, then let's try a serious argument. Consider how an economist might answer the following question using flawless, tight economic logic.

Question: What is the effect of an increase in the value of the pound on unemployment? By the way, the table below is completely humourless but I got a degree in economics 25 years ago and it's about time it was useful for something.

Answer 1
A decrease in the value of the pound means that…
The price of British exports falls which means that…
More foreigners buy more British goods which…
Increases the demand for British goods which means…
British firms take on more workers to meet the extra demand so…
Unemployment *falls*.

Answer 2
A decrease in the value of the pound means that...
The price of foreign imports increases which...
Increases the costs of some of the goods and services which British companies buy which in turn...
Makes British goods more expensive and so fewer people want to buy them and therefore...
British firms don't need as many staff and so...
Unemployment *rises*.

Still not convinced that economics is no more scientific than witchcraft? Then how about this? Only the Government and the banks employ economists. End of.

So, much as we might criticise seismologists for failing to predict a tsunami or volcanologists for not noticing that the simmering cauldron they've been sticking gadgets in for the last 28 years is about to erupt, at least they can explain what happened after the fact. Economists can neither explain nor predict. Economics truly is, in the words of John Stuart Mill, "the dismal science".

But it has managed to construct an impressive ideological edifice. In 1776, Adam Smith published his chef d'oeuvre, "An inquiry into the Nature and Causes of the Wealth of Nations," which defined the prevailing orthodoxy until 1936 when John Maynard Keynes published his magnus opus, "The General Theory on Employment, Interest and Money". These two books have towered over economic theory, interrupted only by the brief flash in the pan of mumbo-jumbo in the 1980s known as monetarism. Smith's laissez-faire capitalism was basically saying, "leave it to the bankers and the 'invisible hand' will sort everything out." In the context of the 2007-8 banking crisis, you have to wonder what sort of hand Smith had in mind – market forces or poker? Anyway Keynesianism overturned this logic to say, "if the bankers lose £10bn, give them another £12bn and see if they can do any better."

Clearly these two elderly ideologies are flawed and out-dated. The world of economics is obviously in desperate need for another great, overarching economic theory. This time one for the twenty-first century, encompassing the inter-linking machinations of the global economy which Smith and Keynes could not foresee.

And here it is!

My next publication will be entitled, "Unsubstantiated Waffle". In this masterpiece, I will not only break with economic tradition by writing a book with a title of fewer than eight words, but I will tackle such disturbing imponderables as what would happen if economists took up forecasting the weather. Obviously the book is backed by a wealth of econometric data but it basically comes down to the following formula:

$Rr = f(B^\wedge b)$

Where R = Risk of recession
       B = the number of banks
       b = the volume of bullshit (measured in boris's)
       $\wedge$ = pretentious mathematical symbol, prerequisite for any self-respecting scientific thesis.

The theory boils down to the fact that the likelihood of economic recession is a factor of a combination of an excessive number of banks and an exponential increase in the volume of bullshit in business.

Really it's all fairly obvious. The number of banks was growing, some of them whose very names should have been causes for concern. For instance, a bank which is an anagram of Satan Nerd (Santander) is pretty worrying. And if banks have names with elementary spelling errors (Citibank), what hope is there that they'll be numerate?

Other banks try to give us a clue in their advertising material – NatWest promote themselves as providing "helpful banking", meaning that they are helping themselves to enormous bonuses. Meanwhile HSBC holds itself out as the "World's local bank" which respects and adapts to local customs. Like outright greed in the finance sector, for instance. If HSBC were a real "local bank", you would have thought by now it would have figured out that most people who have money to deposit in a bank would like that bank to be open on the one day in a week (Saturday) when they've got some spare time to go there.

It didn't matter that, when we walked down the high street, there were nine different shops (i.e. high street banks) all trying to sell us various forms of the same "(something you're scared of) protection insurance" policies which never paid up. (As an aside, how exactly can you ever make a claim for "death-in-service" insurance?) We were comfortable that, regulated by the Financial Services Authority, audited by the "Big 4" accountants and credit-checked by reputable credit agencies, these august organisations wouldn't let us down. We could literally bank on them. We could even forgive them their bonuses and their knighthoods.

What we didn't realise was that bullshit had fatally spread through their profession like a virulent cancer. That the banks were playing pass the parcel with money only instead of taking off a layer of wrapping paper every time the music stopped, they were adding another tier of incomprehensible jargon. Did they know what was going on? Who knows - but next time you go over your overdraft limit, why not give them a taste of their own medicine and blame it on irresponsible lending in the US. And then ask for your overdraft limit to be doubled.

The third variable in my fatuous formula is bullshit. Bullshit is all very well as long as it is confined to safe havens like football commentaries but it can have a disastrous effect when it spews into things that really matter. But, to be balanced, business bullshit is not without its disadvantages, so here's some food for thought on whether or not it might actually help in some areas.

Should Business Bullshit be used...	Advantage of Business Bullshit	Disadvantage of Business Bullshit	Overall conclusion
In Church services?	Business bullshit would fit in nicely because, like Strategic Executives, the laugh-a-minute jolly old Pope emeritus Benedict XVI is a passionate believer in making sure nobody understands a word he says. Consistent with the Christian belief in the resurrection of the Dead, he recently reintroduced Latin into Catholic mass.	Business Bullshit doesn't currently have the range of vocabulary for religious concepts such as humility and forgiveness. Let alone famines, floods and virgins.	X (it's probably best not to inflict a twenty-first century scurge – business bullshit – on an institution still struggling with medieval attitudes to things like homosexuality and women).
In top secret military communications?	Impossible for enemy to de-code.	Impossible for own side to de-code.	X (there's enough friendly fire incidents as it is).
By X-factor judges?	Business bullshit would be a much more humane way of rejecting contestants than watching Simon Cowell tell a wannabe Wag that she's got the looks and talent of a garden slug but then…	Someone's got to put these chavs in their place.	✓ (anything which undermines the appeal of the X-factor is a good thing).

Whatever the pros and cons of business bullshit in the contexts above, what is for sure is that its creeping into the finance sector was catastrophic.

There used to be a maxim that if you owed the bank a few thousand quid, *you* were in trouble but if you owed the bank a few million quid, *the bank* was in trouble. Well what about when the bank owes a few *billion* quid? Well then we're *all* in trouble. Except for Fred Goodwin.

So what can be done? In order to work out a solution, we need to analyse the problem at its core. We need to visit a typical bank branch.

A visit to the bank

Banks like to gamble and encourage this amongst their customers. So, on arrival at the bank, the first gamble is which queue to take. Will it be the long but relatively fast moving "cashier number six please" one, at the end of which you find your "helpful" local banker sitting behind bullet proof glass and with microphones ideally placed for all their 6 year old customers but a bit of a pain for the rest of us. Or the unguarded "customer service desk" the staffing of which appears to be determined by some sort of tombola. Bad luck if you get the one who's never been trained on banking basics and hasn't a clue where anything is. You can spot him by the badge on his lapel. It says, "Branch Manager".

A popular pastime whilst queuing is to rehearse your spiel when eventually your turn comes. Rehearsal is an intrinsic part of queuing – and not just in banks. Some queues are more challenging than others in this respect. For instance, "Antiques Roadshow" attendees need to practise both their "pleasantly surprised at the expert valuation" look (when in fact they're crushingly disappointed) combined with their, "it's priceless in sentimental terms," response.

Another curious feature of bank queues is you come across pens chained to the desk. Despite the fact that the banks lost billions of pounds by willy-nilly giving mortgages to all sorts of no hopers, they seem bizarrely over-prudent when it comes to managing their pens. Perhaps this explains the great mystery of how, over the course of that fateful weekend in September 2008, the banking leaders managed to get the then Chancellor of the Exchequer, Alistair Darling, to dole out another

£400bn to them. "Alistair, we've got some good news and some bad news. The bad news is we seem to have lost £400,000,000,000. The good news is that all our cheap biros are fully accounted for."

The real bummer is when you eventually get to the end of your chosen queue, you're told you have to fix a meeting with your "relationship manager". So there you are – you thought you were coming to the bank to arrange a loan and the bank's decided your marriage is on the rocks.

The future of banking

When governments come across an insoluble and controversial issue, they convene a "full judicial inquiry", which takes ages to write a very boring report. The Government's tactic is to hope that by the time the inquiry publishes its report, everyone will have forgotten the original issue and therefore its recommendations can be ignored. So here are some recommendations which can be ignored regarding banking.

1. Nomenclature

The first thing which needs to change is the term "bank." Post the 2007-8 banking crash, the phrase, "you can bank on it," just doesn't work. In France, the word "bank" is spelt "banque" and pronounced "bonk." This is perfectly apt since they exist to screw us all. So they should all be renamed "bonks." "Royal Bonk of Scotland" – got a nice ring to it, don't you think? Even better – "Royal Bonk of Bagpipes."

Another term which really has to go is the so-called Rights Issue. Arguably the apotheosis of business bullshit, the documents supporting these transactions (audited by accountants and scrutinised by lawyers) take hundreds of pages to say....

Dear Shareholder

We've cocked up and need another £100 million to survive for a couple more weeks, so can you please cough up.

Yours faithfully

Rt.Hon. Field Marshall Lord Barings of Northern Rock KG, CBE, NOBHEAD

---

2. Two birds with one stone

Estimates of the cost of the banking bail-out seem to vary from between £400bn and £850bn. It's mind-boggling that we don't seem to know how much even to the nearest £100bn. Anyway let's call it £600bn. Over what period? Well let's be generous and say it wasn't caused by a group of greedy spivs, cashing in on the de-regulation in the last 30 years. Let's say banks have *always* been losing money, so that's over a 300 year period. That's still £8m *per day*!!!. Of course en route they were rewarded with an assortment of plaudits and honours ("services to banking" or was it "services to self-enrichment"?)

And when it all collapsed, the taxpayer conveniently stepped in to reimburse them, so that they could resume paying themselves bonuses a few months later. Sorry, what I should have said was that if we taxpayers hadn't stepped in, then all those talented bankers would have migrated elsewhere. Shame. I've suddenly thought of how the Government could improve the net migration stats.

Anyway we shouldn't go on about past events – the FSA has now been abolished and it's great to see that its discredited former employees haven't just transferred to the new regulators: well three of them haven't.

3. Deception

Another great act of deception is those letters you get from your helpful, local credit card provider advertising a FREE balance transfer. But wait a moment – what does that footnote in font size Arial 0.0003 say? "Subject to 3% handling charge." There is therefore no way that this can be described as "free". How come banks can get away with this and not other companies? For instance, would a travel agency be able to get away with a promotion like....

> WIN A FREE All-Expenses-Paid* weekend for two in a 5-star hotel in Venice

Thought for the Day

In life, it's important to have self-esteem and dreams and banking provides great solace in these critical areas. Firstly, unlike other professions, where you need to be qualified to be a doctor, lawyer, accountant or teacher, *anyone* can occupy any position in a bank, even if they have the intellect of a contestant on "Family Fortunes". And secondly, however badly you do your job, comfort yourself with the thought that it could never be as badly as the people who ran Britain's banks in the first decade of the twenty-first century. Just try not to think about their bonuses too much.

*by you

BANKERS' GLOSSARY OF TERMS

Term	Meaning
Banker	A term formerly used to refer to a safe bet; contemporary meaning now synonymous with a word it rhymes with.
Bank of England	Should be interpreted literally, i.e. this is the *only* bank in England (the rest are casinos).
Buy short, sell long	A bet
Put option	A risky bet
Derivative	A very risky bet
Sub-prime mortgage	500-1 outsider
Credit Default Swap	Cock-up
Global economy	Banker's betting stake
Non Executive Director	Useless twat
Financial Services Authority (FSA)	An authority which provided services to the financial sector, mainly of a blind eye nature.

Term	Meaning
Quantitative easing	Taxpayer subsidy enabling bankers to place more bets.
Mortgage Adviser	Technical term for a person who got straight Ds at A-level.
Highly talented	The way bankers describe themselves.
International direct debit	Something "highly talented" (q.v.) people haven't yet been able to work out how to do.
Computer blip	Major malfunction caused by decades of mismanagement.
A rights issue	A begging letter
Rogue trader	Banker who gets caught out doing what they're all up to.
Independent Financial Adviser	Bullshitter
IMPORTANT changes to your terms and conditions	Boring "Spot the Difference" competition.

XI

ESSENTIAL OFFICE POLITICS

"All political lives end in failure" – J Enoch Powell

I bet by now you think I'm a real cynic. And if you think my views on economists and bankers in the last chapter were a bit harsh, then what line are you expecting on the subject of this chapter, politicians? Well prepare to be surprised – Karl Marx was pretty positive about some aspects of capitalism and yours sincerely has got a lot of sympathy for politicians!

Two types of people say, "I'm not political" – very political people and bigots. Put another way: people who are very good at politics and people who are very bad at it. Like it or not, politics (etymologically linked to the word "politeness") is the practice of not entirely doing or saying what fully represents your opinion, in the interests of achieving your goal and/or of keeping a team together. After all, we humans are better off working as a team: anyone who disagrees might like to try reverting to being a hunter-gatherer. And yet still this fundamental feature of human life, politics, is denigrated as if it were unambiguously a bad thing. People who leave a job because they want to go, "somewhere less political," are basically saying they want to go somewhere where there are no people. Politics is a feature of human interaction and that is a good thing.

Of course Strategic Executives, who would never dream of making dodgy expense claims or voting themselves nice pay rises, are at the vanguard of people who are cynical about politicians. So let's think about how they would stand up to the scrutiny which politicians are routinely subjected to.

For instance, one of the factors which makes life difficult for politicians is that their every utterance is scrutinised by media and opposition alike and compared to everything they've ever previously said on the subject. God help a politician who says something which contradicts a speech he made 15 years ago. They live in a World where changing your mind is a "humiliating U-turn" and an off-the-cuff joke with your mates is a "gaffe". A white lie to protect a friend borders on corruption.

And as if the life of a politician wasn't hard enough, to cap it all they have to submit to a public vote to get their job!

Wouldn't it be wonderful if freedom of the press and free elections were extended to business? We could hold Strategic Executives to account for their business plan pledges, heckle them when they trot out their customary bullshit and read some investigative journalism on what the hell it is that Quality Managers do all day.

But for a minute let's think about an office with no politics, in which everyone has a Duke of Edinburgh Award for Diplomacy and mindlessly says what he or she really thinks. No backstabbing or backbiting, no two facedness just pure, naked honesty. Is this the sort of place those people who say they want somewhere "less political" would want to work?

THE FUSION OF BUSINESS AND POLITICS CAN BE BAD FOR DEMOCRACY

There now follows a Power Point presentation on behalf of the Strategic Executives Party.

Who would have thought that TV would ever sink lower than Keith Harris and Orville's 1982 Christmas Special!

Tuesday morning; Boss and PA in boss's office

Boss: "Good morning, Laura – have you completed that simple task I've asked you to do about six times? Oh and by the way can you please unbutton your top so that I can get a better view of your bra?"

Secretary (or Executive Assistant or whatever poxy job title they have these days): "I haven't started that work because you only remember about 15% of things you ask me to do and anyway, if you do remember, I thought you'd forgive me if I put on my flirty voice and dressed a bit more scantily."

Boss: "Quite right, I'll forgive you. I only recruited you for your looks. That other trollop would have been much more effective but not so easy on the eye. Anyway what's on my agenda today?"

Secretary: "You're appraising that stuck-up cow of a Project Manager who tried to block my appointment and has been bitching about me ever since. She's hovering outside right now, in that smart outfit she only wears for meetings which she thinks might have a bearing on her payrise."

Boss: "Better show her in."
Project Manager enters.

Boss: "Good morning, Cheryl. My God, you're ugly."

Project Manager: "Good morning, Brian: you seem even smellier and fatter than normal today."

Boss: "How are you? Good weekend? By the way, I'm not in the slightest bit interested in the answer, unless you've got something scandalous or titillating to tell me."

Project Manager: "I had a very dull weekend shopping and watching TV but thought it would enhance my promotion and payrise prospects if I said I'd done something like, 'I spent most of the weekend out jogging or in the gym: I'm in training for the BAI plc triathlon next month and am entering with a team of great business contacts. We're raising money for charity and I might get a few good business leads out of it. A real win-win.' "

Boss : "Now as you know this is the six-monthly review of your objectives, which I have never looked at, not least because I haven't a clue how to find the appraisal form on my computer. If I had managed to find the form, I wouldn't have been able to get into it because I have a strict policy of never remembering any of my passwords. Do you have a hard copy of your objectives so that I can pretend to remember what you should have been doing these last six months?"

Project Manager: "Here you are, you lazy sod."

Boss: "Let me play for time and ask you a few general questions. Whilst I'm not listening to your answers, I can then jot down a few ill-considered prejudices and go through them later. How have the last six months been for you?"

Project Manager: "Very good: I think I have accomplished my over-riding objective of minimising both my hours at work and the work I do whilst covering this up by talking pompously and dressing in a professional manner."

Boss: "I didn't listen to a word of that because I was trying to fathom out what the hell these objectives are on about. What are your current projects?"

Project Manager: "There have been a few projects, none of which have actually achieved anything – firstly, there's the technical one nobody understands; then there's the one I always promise to start but never do and finally there's the one I have started but have collected a selection of convenient excuses for not progressing (no replies to my e-mails requesting information, lack of budget, that sort of thing)."

Boss: "I didn't really understand any of that so let me talk in general terms about your performance with no specific examples to back up what I say. I find you somewhat…..hmm……ugly. Longer term I'm thinking of getting a prettier Project Manager and am thinking that the best way of engineering that is to pretend we're restructuring such that your role would be redundant. Any thoughts about that?"

STRATEGIC EXECUTIVES ARE NOT ALWAYS WELL PREPARED FOR APPRAISAL MEETINGS

Before getting down to the nitty gritty of looking at how you've performed this year in relation to your objectives, can I just clear up one detail? Who the hell are you?

> Project Manager: "If you do that, I'll screw you – not physically, but financially."
>
> Boss: "Before I irrevocably alienate you by firing you, I just need to get something useful out of you. Can you think of anything you could do that would make me look good in front of my bosses?"
>
> Project Manager: "On the assumption that your bosses find you as distasteful as the rest of us, then suicide would be pretty endearing."
>
> Boss: "Well I think this has been a very valuable meeting. Of course I won't do anything such as documenting our discussion or updating your objectives but I will misrepresent a few extracts from our conversation for the purposes of impressing my bosses."

Most offices are more civil than that. On the surface at least. So what we have instead are rather dull conversations with clearly defined rules.

Office conversation in the 21st century

A drawback of office politics is that business conversations are unnecessarily protracted although this does provide the underlying justification for business lunches, unnecessary foreign travel and the like.

Perhaps the delights of speed-dating could be applied to business conversations? Sellers would circulate round tables of buyers asking, "Are you likely to ever buy anything from my company?" "Nope." Move onto the next table. Instead of this we have the elaborate charade of the Strategic Executives' conversation where a rigid code of etiquette has to be followed.

Firstly if the conversation is on the 'phone, it is paramount that the Strategic Executive puts the call on speaker 'phone and turns it up to maximum volume. This has a number of advantages. Firstly it advertises the fact to everyone within earshot that the Strategic Executive is "in action." (When the call starts to go awry, the Strategic Executive will hastily grab the handset.) Secondly it gives the appearance that the Strategic Executive is multi-tasking. In fact they can't really uni-task but by being on the squawk box, they give the appearance that whilst rambling away, they're also attending to some high-profile document or other.

The conversation also follows an elaborate protocol. Strategic Executives do not talk about the weather (very pleb) or anything remotely interesting. Their opening gambit is therefore usually something like, "keeping busy?" Even if a Strategic Executive has spent all month picking his nose and wondering why the crispy bogeys are more tasty than the slimy ones, he will never admit to things being anything other than, "a bit hectic right now," or, "there's a lot going on." The follow-up question is, "how's business?" The answer to this

WHEN FACED WITH A DIFFICULT QUESTION, STRATEGIC EXECUTIVES OFTEN DEPLOY THEIR "YOU MUST HAVE THE WRONG NUMBER" ROUTINE

question must be upbeat. Even the Strategic Executive of a powdered wigs manufacturer (last recorded sale, 1821) would say, "picking up."

Then it's time to talk about the general state of the economy. The first point a Strategic Executive makes needs to be prefaced by the remark, "there was an article in the FT today about…." This outright lie will not be refuted since nobody actually reads the FT (the last person who tried lapsed into a vegetative state after three paragraphs). Hence the piles of pristine FTs which accumulate in posh receptions. In fact if you try to open one, you'll find you can't, it's just a pink slab of mush.

Preamble out of the way, it's now time to get down to the real meat of the call. It doesn't take long. In fact it doesn't take at all because at this point the Strategic Executive will realise that he actually has nothing of substance to say. So the 'phone call needs to be promptly aborted. A bit like watching an episode of "Lost" - no sooner have the opening credits finished, then you're off to the commercial break. Again the objective is to appear busy so something like, "my 8.30's arrived," or, "I'm already 30 minutes behind schedule," is the traditional closing.

Meeting-speak

At least 'phone calls can be abruptly terminated and the Strategic Executive extricates himself from his famous John Major impersonation (long period in office, nothing to show for it). Meetings, however, are another kettle of fish and, so the Strategic Executive has developed a few one-liners to cover for their lack of progress and knowledge.

What they say	What they mean
"Can we discuss this off-line?"	"Out of sheer prejudice I completely disagree with what you have just said but I need time to work out a counter-argument."
"I'm waiting to hear back from Brian."	"Two minutes ago, I realised I'd done sod-all about this action point I received six weeks ago, so I've just sent out a scrambled e-mail to Brian."
"All comments are welcome."	"as long as they're complimentary."

Living with politics

So if we accept that there needs to be office politics in order to avoid complete dysfunctional breakdown, here are a few tricks of the trade.

The golden rule of office politics is…..little drumroll…… *make it look like you have done something well when you basically know that you either have really screwed it up or, more commonly, haven't done it all.*

1. Jargonista

When in trouble use technical jargon or, if you're very skilled at this, completely made-up words, as long as they are multi-syllabic. A great example of this is TV adverts for skincare which rely on references to chemical ingredients nobody has ever heard of and show men in white laboratory coats poring over their microscopes in an attempt to convince gullible viewers that their latest flavoured soap really can, "knock a decade off you." This technique can be transported into a business, so Strategic Executives rely upon identifying some sort of spurious specialism nobody else understands and then using impenetrable jargon to overstate its importance and implications.

Another technique under this heading is to make up some nonsensical mumbo-jumbo and pretend it's a quote by Shakespeare that supports your line of argument. Shakespeare was in many ways a forerunner of business bullshit in that he managed to come up with stuff which nobody understands but everyone reveres.

2. Sybilisms

This takes its name from the sketch in the 1970s TV sit-com "Fawlty Towers" when hapless hotel manager Basil suggests his wife appears on Mastermind, "Sybil Fawlty; specialist subject, 'the bleeding obvious'."

The technique involves thinking of something that's readily apparent to all and sundry but then appearing intelligent by stating that we shouldn't do the opposite. For example you'd look stupid if your contribution to an office meeting was, "we should all stay alive." But what about if you were to say, "we should avoid any possibility that any one of us might conceivably be at the risk of losing their lives"? Much more profound.

Another variant is the foreign sybilism, also known as "le sybilisme" or "el sybillissimo", namely the statement of the obvious but in a foreign language in order to make it sound very clever. For example, rather than blandly saying that we need to improve so as to get things done just in time, try saying that we're going to deploy the Japanese techniques of Kaizen and Kanban. Like Ant and Dec nobody knows which one's which but they've been getting away with it for years.

A more sophisticated variant is the so-called "reverse sybilism". This involves coming out with an absurd rhetorical question nobody will refute. "Does anyone in this room think that, if we really put our minds to it, we can't be No.1 in the World?"

3. Miscellaneous

Here's a word which Strategic Executives are killing off – "miscellaneous". Not only does it suffer from the drawback of comprising five syllables but it implies that what follows doesn't matter so much and is insignificant. And of course everything a Strategic Executive says or writes is "key". Anything but miscellaneous. So here are a few non-key ways of looking good when completely ineffective.

- Grow a goatee beard (especially if you have a chubby face which needs to look sharp).

- Always agree with the boss. The art is to find out what the boss thinks and then heartily agreeing with him, without making it to obvious that's what you're up to. Remember that honest opinions in business are a bit like farts – it's best to keep them in, but once they're out, deny them.

- Hope that your BlackBerry rings and then you can scuttle off muttering something melodramatic like, "this could be big."

The Mother of all excuses

Even making use of these deflection techniques, from time to time every Strategic Executive has to explain why he has done sweet FA.

Train and tube services have perfected the art of blaming delays on inanimate objects – signal failure, points failure, leaves on the track, wrong type of snow, etc. In extreme cases they seem to think they can get away with us all believing in a Thomas the Tank Engine world where trains have a mind of their own – "rolling stock is in the wrong place." The point to note is that they never blame it on humans, i.e. it's never a case of "driver overslept", "piss-poor maintenance of the signal" or "crap management."

Strategic Executives also have a repertoire for blaming inanimate objects - "my computer's crashed and I've lost all my data" being a familiar refrain. But the Strategic Executives real speciality is blaming other people at the earliest opportunity, or poka-yoke as it is called in Japanese. The business world has taken the blame-game way beyond crude finger-pointing and concocted the ultimate recipe for utter confusion and a total absence of accountability. It is called matrix management.

Matrix management has come about because the business world has decided to answer a tricky question with a trick answer. "Who should be your line manager - the guy who runs your function, the one in charge of your office or the one responsible for your market sector?" Answer: "All of them." Hence the cocktail of confusion which is matrix management. A completely ridiculous and impracticable system of dotted reporting lines, shared objectives and a world in which everyone can call themselves a manager and nobody's a managee. The people who failed to organise the proverbial piss-up in a brewery were operating a matrix management system. Imagine if an army went into battle with each soldier receiving contradictory instructions from different generals and you have the essence of the consequences of matrix management.

But the beauty of this system is that nobody knows what anybody is doing and so those who are doing nothing can pretend they are doing something for someone. And so the Strategic Executive lives on. Brilliant.

XII

AT LARGE

So far we have concentrated on the Strategic Executive in good old Blighty. Like Americans, we have ignored the fact that there's a world beyond our borders. In so doing, we are omitting a key aspect of the Strategic Executive's life and one with the scope for huge entertainment and confusion (and not much work). So let's look at how the "work" of a Strategic Executive – unproductive in his own country – becomes utterly counter-productive when he strays abroad.

The Strategic Executive in transit

Some things in life are utterly pointless – for instance forecasting the end of the World. If you're wrong, you look like a fruitcake; if you're right, everyone dies so you don't get any credit. Similarly pointless are Strategic Executive trips overseas.

The build-up to the Strategic Executive's foreign business trip all centres around how he can get a Business class seat when company policy requires economy (or "coach" as the Americans rather confusingly call it). A variety of tactics are deployed – the "free upgrade" which he loses in his expense claim or the old "only seats available were in business" line being amongst the most common.

Once inside the airport terminal, there's a limit to how long you can pass the time playing, "Spot the thin American," so the venue represents one of those locations where the Strategic Executive imagines he might be able to act out one of his childish fantasies, the so-called "elevator pitch." This is the 30 second spiel that businessmen are meant to be able to churn out upon having a chance encounter with a bigwig from a prospective client and only having a limited amount of time to sell their company. Putting to one side the fact that few lifts could physically support the bulk of two Strategic Executives, what likelihood is there that this scenario will ever arise? Lifts are one of two places (tubes being the other one) where no matter how closely pressed you are to someone else, it is paramount NOT to make any conversation whatsoever. Let alone, "Come on, let's hear your elevator pitch then."

Having boarded the 'plane and overcome the temptation to masquerade as a vegetarian (they always get served first), this is where Business Class seats come into their own. You may have paid ten times the price but you get an exemption from the great Battle for Possession of the Arm-rests which are fought day-in, day-out on hundreds of flights. The Strategic Executive is a formidable opponent in this battle, able to deploy a number of tactics. First amongst these is obesity, i.e. some Strategic Executives are so fat that their stomach just cascades over the arm-rests. Game over. Less well endowed Strategic Executives need to resort to other tactics. Getting out the laptop and spraying their elbows out like an albatross in flight is a popular one. Another tactic is to launch a barrage of snorts, grunts, coughs and sneezes which drive their neighbours, fearing for their health, into a hasty retreat. After all, the concession of arm-rest space is a small price to pay for your good health. But, if all else fails, the Strategic Executive has one secret weapon sure to drive away his opponent– conversation…

Strategic Executives often take aisle seats, meaning that they can prey on couples. Starting out on their dream holiday or even more pitiably their honeymoons, imagine the poor couple sharing their hopes and aspirations for the future and then all of sudden up pipes their neighbour with his ice-breaker opening line, "See that airline catering firm out there? They could benefit from what I've done at BAI plc, transforming the business by shifting from a traditional, mono-silo oriented paradigm to a flexible, cross-dimensional end-user focussed model."

Nicely snuggled in, the Strategic Executive then has to endure one of the two bits of the flight he really hates, take-off (landing is the other one). This is a particularly stressful time for the Strategic Executive. Not because he is scared of flying. But because he has to turn off his BlackBerry.

Once the 'plane has landed but before the "fasten your seat belts" sign turns off, the Strategic Executive turns his BlackBerry back on like a heroine addict grasping his last fix. At this stage he somewhat inexplicably stands up and gets his luggage out of the overhead hold. Why airline passengers do this is a complete mystery because whoever stands up first, whoever gets off the plane first, you all end up standing around together waiting for the luggage carousel in the baggage reclaim area.

Baggage reclaimed and having spent the taxi ride making superfluous and unsociable 'phone calls purely designed to show off his cosmopolitan, 24/7 lifestyle, the Strategic Executive checks into his hotel. He instantly feels at home surrounded by the cast of clones which comprises the international business hotel clientele.

International business hotels are full of all sorts of gadgets to justify their excessive prices, e.g. lifts with a mind of their own, room light dimmers, bewildering shower controls, a multitude of soap bottles with indecipherably small writing on their labels and phone consoles like the NASA control room. You really could benefit from someone explaining how all these knobs, buttons and levers work but do they show you? Do they hell? The one thing they do for you in this technological jamboree is a flunky comes to your room to "turn up" your bed. As if you could master the shower, telephone and blinds and then be left wondering, "how exactly do I get into bed?"

The Strategic Executive abroad

The objective of the Strategic Executive abroad is to try to ignore that he is in a foreign country – he'll do his damnedest to get the nearest thing to an English breakfast, will expect English TV channels and restaurant service and show no interest whatsoever in foreign customs, culture or places of interest. But most of all he will relentlessly speak English. We English complacently assume that it is acceptable for us to approach a foreigner in his own country and address him in our mother tongue as if he were our butler. But how would the Strategic Executive react if the tables were turned and on the streets of London he were to be suddenly accosted by a stranger greeting him with the words "Parlez-vous français? Pourquoi es-tu un buffoon?"

To be fair, most Strategic Executives do make the effort to learn a few foreign phrases like "good morning", "please" and "thank you" which is highly ironic because they never use these terms in England.

But the obstacles to the Strategic Executive's mission to anglicise the rest of the world are many and varied. Here are the main ones.

1   Dates

One cause of constant confusion is how the date is written. Whereas we Brits record the date as DD/MM/YY, the Chinese go for YY/MM/DD and the Americans record it as MM/DD/YY so in USA, July 27 is 7/27 and not 27/7. Imagine arriving back from work after your Christmas and New Year break, you pick up an e-mail from your American boss saying that you need to complete some monstrous task by 1/2. Don't sit back and think you've got a whole month because he doesn't mean 1st February, he means today!!!

If in doubt about your US deadline, remember the simple rule that Americans think they can do anything from stuffing themselves on 12 Big Macs to conquering a Middle Eastern country within 24 hours and that you should be able to match them. So, if you work for an American company and you estimate something's going to take two weeks, don't say that, they'll fire you. You have two options. Either you can say that it'll be done in a fortnight. This is the perfect response because the word "fortnight" is not in their dictionary and they hate admitting they don't know something. "Sorry, didn't you know that "fortnight" means six months?" Or, play them at their own game: say that you'll finish it tomorrow. When tomorrow comes, say you'll have it done the following day and so on and so on until it takes two weeks. Astonishingly Americans much prefer someone who's keen but keeps failing, to someone who appears lazy by accurately predicting that something will take longer than their 24-hour maximum deadline horizon.

There are, however, some rogue Americans who have noticed that the "American Way" is not universal and that other parts of the world have different languages, currencies and time zones and are not populated exclusively by Al-Qaeda suicide bombers. They realise that a "cell" is the basic unit of bio-material which can have a life of its own and not a mobile phone (although perhaps on reflection, there's not much difference).

2   Time

An appendage of the dates confusion is that Americans have no idea what the expression "half past 8" means, let alone it's more confusing contraction "half eight." They always say, "8.30." So if you want to make an American waste a few hours, tell him that the meeting starts at, "half 12," and he'll turn up 6½ hours early at 6 o'clock.

A nice little twist on the time thing is that the Americans tend to put their clocks forward one hour two weeks earlier than the Europeans and there's one state (Arizona) which boycotts the whole clock-changing ritual. Of course this is all lost on the majority of Americans, who, thinking that "time difference" is a reference to a satellite delay, are continually impressed by Europeans who pitch up for work at 4 a.m., although they have noticed that we don't get much done after lunch.

3   Divided by the same language

The American assault on the English language has several facets: firstly they hate multi-syllabic words, so aluminium for instance has become aluminum.

Then they completely change the meaning of words - they call braces "suspenders", their "pavement" is a road and if they ask you if you, "wanna pop?" it doesn't mean they think you're as fat as they are to the point of bursting, they're actually offering you a fizzy drink. And of course, even if you are sitting comfortably at home, you are labelled as an "international" person: Americans are the only people who can describe themselves as "domestic".

In America, the company boss is known as the "President" and his senior direct reports as "Vice Presidents". It's like calling a Managing Director "Prime Minister" or "King". One advantage of this pompous nomenclature from a British standpoint is that the job title "director" is not particularly prestigious over there, so UK subsidiaries of US companies can have loads of them.

4   Bank holidays

We British really are crap at bank holidays. It's not that we don't have enough of them, it's just that we haven't worked out what half of them are for. The Spring Bank holiday and the one at the end of August mark no occasion and the May Day one marks international labour day, as if we were some great socialist nation.

Most other countries have no such problems with various Independence Days and Catholic holidays marking the comings and goings of the Virgin Mary & Son. The Catholic church can often be relied upon to come up with a bank holiday on a Thursday, which is much the most civilised day of the week for one since it completely sabotages the following Friday as a working day.

Meanwhile a couple of orthodox countries have kept the Julian calendar which means they can doss their way through two Christmases – one when *they* are on holiday; another when everyone else is. However some of the choices of reasons for bank holidays do smack of desperation – for instance the Dutch have a bank holiday to mark the birthday of Queen Juliana which is very touching except that she died in 2004. More bizarre is the fact that the only two countries which mark what we call VE day (the end of the Second World War) with a holiday are the French (who pathetically capitulated) and the Italians who were on the wrong side for seven years, swapped sides when the outcome was a near-certainty and now claim to have won it.

International thought for the day

One of the features of international travel is the choice of destinations. Strategic Executives love all things big and superficial so Dubai, with its "7-star" hotels, fits the bill nicely. But how can you explain China as a favourite destination? Living in Beijing must be a bit like being Keith Richards – you live your life in a total haze. So what could attract Strategic Executives there – apart from the fact that the Chinese own half the capitalist world? Is it the Chinese's defence of liberal democracy and human rights? Or their environmental credentials? Or could it just be that the hotel staff politely bow when a Strategic Executive passes by?

So if the Strategic Executive can do a bit of cross-border harm, let's now go even wider. What damage can he do to the planet?

XIII

GAS EMISSIONS – STRATEGIC EXECUTIVES AND THE ENVIRONMENT

What colour do you associate with a Strategic Executive? It's an easy question for the Ice Queen of HR: blue for her heart but for a Strategic Executive there's a wide range of choices. Pink to represent the disgusting open-neck shirt he wears on Dress-down Fridays in an attempt to look cool; yellow and black – nature's traditional "danger" colours; red for the embarrassment he should feel but never does and, of course, excremental brown for the quality of his written work. Well, the colour he likes to associate with himself is "green" – not green for the envy we all feel that these guys are so well-paid or green for his naïvety in believing we all think he's a great guy, but green for his environmental credentials. In one of mankind's greatest acts of hypocrisy, Strategic Executives want to be seen as eco-saviours who have squared the circle of combining business leadership with respect for the environment.

In reality business's attitude to the environment is best encapsulated by the BP Gulf of Mexico oil spill saga. That they managed to make a hole in the floor of the ocean was just about forgivable – they were after all exploring, looking for oil. The fact that it then took three months to resolve was less excusable and some of the attempts to stem the flow would have been comical, had it not been for the damage to the environment. The first attempt was to put some sort of "cap" over the leak – a perfectly sensible idea except that the "cap" looked like some discarded church bell that they'd bought on e-bay the day after the leak. Then they seemed to relocate the set and props from "Total Wipeout" constructing a whole series of water features doomed to failure. Chief

Executive Tony Hayward honourably resigned, his £12m pay-off small compensation from a company whose losses he'd built up to £11bn.

At an individual level, it's fair to say that Strategic Executives do not have a carbon footprint: they have a carbon crater. Whilst a lot of their rhetoric exudes environmental friendliness, sustainable development and going green, the reality is that these characters are one-man mini-Chernobyls spewing out environmental hazards wherever they go. Here are some of the main causes:

1.   Company cars

It is well documented that a Strategic Executive believes that showing off his car is a proxy for flaunting his penis. The love of the company car goes far beyond this – after all Strategic Executives are not in the habit of drawing attention to their genitals in the way that they do their cars (the BBC in the 1970s excepted). Company cars have an extraordinary effect on Strategic Executives. Just as a leap day is the one time in four years when women are allowed to propose to men, so the day that a Strategic Executive gets to choose his new company car is one on which all norms are reversed. If he applied his usual slapdash approach to this subject, he would randomly open a car brochure, stick a pin in and be just as likely to come up with Fiat Panda as his trademark 4x4. But by some mystical process, in choosing his new car, the Strategic Executive suddenly shows skills hitherto lacking. Attention to detail as he meticulously researches all the vehicle's optional extras and numeracy in assessing the tax implications and fuel economy rates of his potential new dick, sorry, car.

Perhaps this love of company cars is due to the fact that these wagons bear striking similarities to the Strategic Executives...

Firstly, cars are past their best after three years; have an average life span of 13 years and in the meantime require increasingly high maintenance. Plus cars have a number of entirely superfluous features. What is the point of a car which can travel at 228 m.p.h. when the speed limit is less than a third of that? Why be able to accelerate from 0 to 60 in 2.8 seconds when you're in a 30 m.p.h. speed limit and stuck behind a V-reg Vauxhall Cavalier? And what is the point of 4-wheel drive when you spend all day shuffling around the M25? Likewise what is the point of being able to churn out e-mails which are destined for the delete-on-delivery treatment and PowerPoint slides so boring that, like the sun, nobody can bear glimpsing at them for more than a nano-second.

Driving with a Strategic Executive is an experience which they are very keen to impose on work colleagues in order to impress them with the size of their cock, I mean, car. Strategic Executives believe that buses and tubes are for losers and they are too lazy and/or fat to waddle anywhere, so in the car we go.

Setting off is a bit painful: firstly the Strategic Executive has to rapidly hide away all the debris which has accumulated on the front passenger seat and which completely undermines the image of himself which he likes to portray to the world (James Blunt CD cover, a copy of the "Sunday Sport" and a couple of used children's nappies). When eventually the ignition key is turned on, the on-board computer suddenly produces a delightful image of the dog turd which has been deposited behind the car. The Strategic Executive commences the protracted programming of the Sat Nav route which he will subsequently choose to ignore. Having managed to convince the machine that he would prefer to communicate in English and not "Espanol" he quickly narrows down his choice of 47 Park Roads to the one he wants and away we go.

The journey takes in the full repertoire of the car's gimmicks. Such as the seat heaters which give their passengers the sensation that they have wet themselves. Or the "eco-driving indicator", an expensive way of telling the driver to go at 55 m.p.h. Of course if such an indicator really could act against environmental hazards, it would quickly activate the driver ejector seat.

The drive itself takes in the Strategic Executive's innovative interpretation of the Highway Code....

Please drive this way   Bruce Forsyth in the vicinity

Accelerate

Barge out, tooting your horn

Cause an accident

Shout obscenities at fellow drivers on account of their slow driving

Drive like this

If only he'd ignore this warning

2. Unnecessary flights

Jetting round the world is a defining feature of the modern Strategic Executive. The idea that his physical presence is fundamental to the success of any particular project is a critical part of his ego and persona. It is also a load of tosh. Not only do modern forms of technology render being there in person superfluous but the Strategic Executive's physical presence at the best of times is a minor hindrance; after a long flight, it's a major irritant.

To simulate the effect of how an air journey affects your effectiveness at work, why not practise this at home? Firstly instead of going to bed at your normal time, line up your least favourite armchair a couple of feet behind the sofa. Then, whilst wearing your work clothes and a silly pair of socks, sit in the said armchair, bumping about for anything between 6 and 13 hours. Eat some re-heated microwave food and watch a couple of crappy films on a TV with a speckly picture and poor sound quality. And then go to work!

Plane journeys do, however, afford an opportunity for one of the Strategic Executive's favourite pastimes – sending out superfluous e-mails from his nice cosy business-class seat. Business-class is a spectacular waste of somebody else's money. The mere name "business" class gives the game away: only a business would spend its money on this form of travel, nobody would dream of frittering away their own hard-earned cash on it. The only real advantage of business-class is that you can lay horizontal and therefore have a reasonable chance of getting some sleep. In this way, at an altitude of 34,000 feet, the Strategic Executive is able to simulate his work on the ground.

3. Team meetings

Social anthropologists will point out that any group above the size of five or six is an ineffective decision-making team. Never mind, let's not let that get in the way of a good piss-up and an opportunity for Strategic Executives to act out their Churchillian fantasies by summoning their underlings to a "summit", "retreat" or "symposium" and kidding themselves that their speeches inspired the masses.

To exacerbate the impact on the environment, now we need to choose a location: somewhere mutually convenient presumably? Oh no, somewhere hundreds or, better still, thousands of miles away is ideal. That way, everyone can waste a day getting there and a day getting back, as well as the three days in the middle which were always going to be a waste of time wherever the meeting was held.

4   Flatulence

The discovery that farting is bad for the O-zone is the great Achilles heel of ecologists in that it enables human dinosaurs to claim that a field of cows is causing as much damage to the planet as their company car fleet of BMW X5s. Why try to reduce one but do nothing about the other? Except the line of argument that cows harm the environment as much as company cars hasn't factored in the carbon emissions emanating from the drivers themselves. What a strange gap in scientific knowledge that we haven't recorded how much we fart.

Of course such research is easier said than done. How do you think Strategic Executives will respond to the question, "how often do you fart?" Honestly? Come off it – they can't even count how many chins they've got, let alone quantify the frequency and strength of their anal emissions. Although the idea of herding Strategic Executives into a remote Scottish field and fitting them with fartometers is quite appealing, dream on, this aspect of the Strategic Executives' activities is likely to go unmeasured for some time yet.

5. Superfluous paperwork

Some things in life are instantly recognisable and yet indescribable. For example, we can all recognise the voices of our family and friends but would we be able to describe them? Something else indescribable is the boredom experienced whilst reading the documents churned out by Strategic Executives. But it's not the contents so much as the sheer volume of this crap which is having an impact on the environment. Deforestation is fine as long as it means getting Russell Brand to have a decent shave and haircut but not when it entails the transformation of Amazon rainforests into papers on, "unparalleled business results arising from a proof of concept methodology which delivers competitive advantage via cross-fertilisation and….," you get the drift.

6. Fitness

It would help the environment considerably if we reduced consumption and made a bit more of an effort to become fit and healthy. Instead we seem hell-bent on making our towns and cities resemble a mass audition as extras in "Shameless".

Fitness is a real problem area for Strategic Executives because, although they can pretend to be efficient, experienced and knowledgeable, they are completely unable to disguise the fact that they are fat. How long can it be before travelators are fitted in offices to transport Strategic Executives from their offices direct to the lifts? Management by walking about can become Management by conveyor belt. In their forlorn War on Weight, they have found unlikely allies in the form of Health & Safety Officers.

Health & Safety officers are amongst the many great misnomers in the business world: you'd think from their title that they protect health and safety. In fact, they go completely over the top on safety and do

zilch about health. So whereas they train you meticulously on the correct technique for avoiding breaking your back whilst replenishing the photocopier's paper supply, what are they doing about the fact that half the office stuffs itself on Big Mac's every day? And whilst they ban social events like Secret Santa on the grounds that staff might suffer RSI pulling presents from the sack, they pursue their insatiable obsession with ergonomically designed chairs, which encourage us to lounge around all day every day. And then they warn you about the numerous hazards and toxins which seem to surround printer cartridges, but quite happily sit and watch as their colleagues sign up to the Presley Diet (peanut butter and sleeping pills leading to a fatal heart attack at 42 whilst sitting on the loo).

7. Bogeys

It is commonly believed that Strategic Executives' contribution to recycling is restricted exclusively to clichés, old ideas, other people's ideas, tired excuses and even third-hand bullshit. In fact they are also assiduous recyclers of one particular form of green waste, bogeys. Problem is that they haven't got the hang of making use of the green recycling bins, preferring to randomly flick their little creations around their offices and cars. Well at least they lose a bit of weight and get a bit of exercise.

For an activity so ancient and widespread as nose-picking, there are very few Self-Help (or should that be Self-Pick?) guides. Until now.

Bogeys come in basically two forms: there are the crusty, dry ones which tend to form when you have a cold and the day-to-day slimy ones which are more readily available. There are three stages to nose-picking: excavation, compilation and disposal. Or, in economic parlance, mining, manufacturing and fly-tipping. Mining is the act of excavating the bogey from its formation site, manufacturing is moulding the raw material into a spherical projectile which can progress to the disposal stage, flicking it at the Ice Queen.

The crusties are much less likely to cause embarassment: they can be quickly excavated and then effortlessly flicked away when the Strategic Executive sees a handshake coming his way. But the slimies are much more incriminating. Their chewing gum characteristics mean that in abruptly trying to end the bogey compilation stage, you can end up with what looks like a long green piece of spaghetti connecting your index finger to your nose. Even worse - at the disposal stage, they

VERY CONVENIENTLY, GOLFING PARLANCE IS READILY TRANSFERABLE TO THE OFFICE ENVIRONMENT

can become impossible to flick away, annoyingly reappearing on the nail that tried to dismiss them. Now think back to your handshakes with Strategic Executives – haven't you noticed a lump which seems strangely slimy? Gross.

8. Prolonged taxi journeys

The only form of public transport that the Strategic Executive will deign to use is taxis. Since the company's paying, the over-riding objective of a corporate taxi journey is to maximise the charge. So keep the cab waiting 25 minutes before getting in. Bring unnecessary luggage with you. Upon arrival, sit in the cab for a further ten minutes making a superfluous 'phone call. Not forgetting the extravagant tip which he wouldn't dream of paying if it were his own money.

The Grey Squirrel theory of the rise of Strategic Executives

From an environmental standpoint, biodiversity is very important. The Strategic Executive is a great threat to diversity since they all want to be the same, they all copy each other and they even try to look like each other. How has this happened? Some ground-breaking research from the Drey school of Stratostudies has come up with a thought provoking natural world parallel which explains the rise of the Strategic Executive at the expense of the species it is gradually replacing, homo sapiens.

We are brought up to believe that squirrels are cuddly little animals which hibernate. Well unless a sub-species has evolved in London N11, I can confirm that they are ingenious and greedy pests and spend as much time asleep in Winter as a newborn baby.

In the UK, Grey Squirrels are directly responsible for the spectacular decline in numbers of the native Red Squirrels in recent years. The Greys are not only more drab in colour but fatter and American. They have rendered the native Reds almost extinct not by directly attacking them but by monopolising their habitat, eating all their food and driving the Reds away. It is now quite common to see them out and about in parks, gardens and forests. There have even been reported sightings of Greys driving 4x4s on the M4. In the rare havens where the Reds survive such as Brownsea Island, nature conservationists will shoot on sight any Grey Squirrel which dares to encroach into this rare bastion of the Reds.

In the context of the rise of Strategic Executives - sounds a bit familiar, doesn't it? Fat Americans eating all the food. And it does explain why, if you ask a Strategic Executive where he's going on holiday this summer, one answer you're not going to hear is, "Brownsea Island."

The solution

For the solution to the Strategic Executive problem, particularly in the context of environmental issues, it may suffice only to look at how the mining sector is dealing with the problem of carbon emissions.

Carbon emissions are wasteful and bad for the environment. Like shit, they are the unnecessary bi-product of interactions which produce something useful. The European Union has therefore introduced legislation limiting the number of carbon emissions any company can have. These are called quotas. If a company exceeds its quota of carbon emissions, it is heavily fined. The effect of this legislation has been to dramatically reduce the number of carbon emissions in the European Union.

Now re-read the paragraph above and replace the words "carbon emissions" with "Strategic Executives".

Voilà – there it is: the solution.

XIV

TURNING THE TABLES

This chapter is for the Strategic Executives because, although they have been the butt of most of the attempts at humour in this book, they do not command a monopoly of the ridiculousness of the office environment. In fact you could say that the fact that they have got themselves into a position where they command an inflated salary whilst doing little more than swanning around emitting vacuous comments and e-mails, whereas everyone else is on a lower pay-rate doing more menial work, is proof positive that it is the "juniors" who are laughable.

Actually the concept of office "juniors" is more or less extinct nowadays since in keeping with universal multiple A*s in GCSEs and widespread first class honours degrees, the general tendency for anyone with half a brain is to totally by-pass any junior level and enter at manager level. It is now quite common for people with the manager job title to have nobody or nothing to manage (like Rebekah Brooks at the moment).

Those people that are junior and choose not to play the business bullshit charade game have reached the glass ceiling because of the following career-blockers.

1. Being too sensible

The way to get on in your career is not to do a great job so much as to *appear* to be doing a great job. A key aspect of this is to *appear* keen. This takes the form of accepting implausible deadlines and onerous tasks with a smile and a "yes, I can" mentality. To Bush a previous US president's quote, "ask not what your company can do for you, ask what you can do for your company," is the dictum you need to be seen to be complying with. Strategic Executives can respond with all manner of "yes sir, no sir" rubbish and general obsequiousness, although, "Great hat, Eugenie" at William and Kate's wedding might have been a bit too far even for them. By contrast, office juniors tend to take a more sensible but entirely self-defeating stance on such matters. They really don't understand that if they stopped whinging about a few minor irritants about their job, they may in future get better rewards enabling them to completely move away from the source of the problem. Here are a couple of things we should all just grin and bear:

- Air conditioning. Air conditioning is designed to work in open plan, homogenous temperature areas. Therefore such anomalies as partitioned offices or sunny days cause it to blow unduly cold or hot in isolated areas. Trying to get this corrected is like 'phoning up British Gas to come and repair your boiler on the grounds that it won't beam you up to the moon. Basically there is no technological solution, so just deal with it.

- "My chair isn't good for my back." Well nor is binge drinking in high heeled shoes, slouching in front of the telly and unusual sex positions, but you don't go round griping about that.

2. Exodus

Leaving at bang-on 5p.m. Unlike Strategic Executives, who disguise the fact that they work less than a 40 hour week by various "dental appointments," "customer visits" and "working from home" (an activity which is about as congruous as, "ironing from the garden" or "swimming in the desert"), office juniors ostentatiously march out at 5p.m. on the dot having equally conspicuously arrived at 9 a.m.

3. Boredom

Looking conspicuously bored during meetings and training sessions. Stifling yawns and avoiding falling asleep are basic business skills which office juniors should learn. Covering your hand with your mouth is the most obvious one but if you are ever caught in full yawn, try to convert it into an expression of jaw-dropping astonishment at the brilliance of what you have just heard. You can practise these techniques at home by simulating interest whilst watching grass grow, paint dry or watching an episode of "Big Brother live".

    4.   Inertia

Complete inability to change. Whereas Strategic Executives have a number of corny clichés about their attitude to change, ("the only thing in life which is certain is change", "it's not necessary to change - survival is not mandatory"), office juniors do become unduly attached to their little ruts. They're a bit like the old geezer who, on seeing his first motor vehicle at the start of the twentieth century, says, "actually I prefer my old job when I used to collect the dung from the horses pulling the Brougham carriage."

    5.   Ingratitude

Ingratitude for the rare acts of kindness which employers bestow. For instance, complaining about the loos being too far away at the Christmas party. Come on, the company's laid on free drink, free food and free music and all you can think about is a walk that's about one-fifth the length of the one you're quite happy to take for a fag break at regular intervals during the course of the working day.

So you either play the game and advance your career or you sit there making reasonable comments about unreasonable aspects of work and watch as people younger and less able than you get the payrises, promotions and trips to glamorous locations.

Revenge

There are two infamous work-related areas, however, where office juniors get their revenge. When basic body functions bring the Strategic Executives crashing down from their hallowed perch. The first of these great levellers is the annual Christmas party...

Office Christmas parties

There is a widespread belief that the office Christmas party is the one occasion in the year when normally sensible people let their hair down a bit too much and end up so pissed that you can't make head nor tail of what they are saying. In fact, in the case of the Strategic Executive, it is the complete opposite: having spent the whole year uttering incomprehensible mumbo-jumbo, they suddenly become coherent. But only for a small part in one evening of the year: the office Christmas party. You have to get them after the alcohol has got rid of the business-speak veneer but before it has reverted them to their normal state, i.e. spouting gibberish. Although, as crapologists will explain, at this later stage of the festivities, their crap moves away from its traditional blend of premeditated, pseudo-intelligent rubbish masquerading as wisdom to a form of speech not dissimilar to railway station announcements when the PA system's on the blink.

Therefore for office juniors and trainee Strategic Executives to get that moment of Strategic Executive coherence, timing is everything. This is the big chance to get in there and find out what he really thinks or indeed whether or not he can think at all. To assist in this, here's the Ready Reckoner to be used to work out, "How drunk is your Strategic Executive?"

Stage	Conversational content	Behavioural features	Usefulness
Stage 1: Bullshit as usual	Still in office mode, talking about how he has leveraged the value-add disconnect in a multi-matrix management environment to aggressively drive up sustainable game changing initiatives.	Always turns up in tired, crumpled suit he's worn all day so by the end of the evening he bears more than a passing resemblance to a "Dr Who" monster contrived by the BBC special effects department in the 1970s.	To be avoided.
Stage 2 ; Egotistical bragging	"I once bumped into Kate Middleton"….(on actoutyourfantasies.com)	Shows off his multi-tasking skills by simultaneously eating and talking, thus becoming a human seed-sower as he liberally sprays partly digested food over his audience, whose names he only gets right 15% of the time.	Will buy plenty of drinks at this stage.
Stage 3: Career advice	Basically the Strategic Executive's career advice boils down to, "Be like me." The gravitas of his message is somewhat undermined by the wearing of a Xmas cracker paper hat and a "Screw me I'm strategic" badge.	Most likely to dance at this stage although for a person claiming to have been at the vanguard of the punk revolution, he shows a remarkable familiarity with the words and actions accompanying Blacklace's "Agadoo."	Will recall the evening but only in fragments so insult him; he'll blame someone else

Stage	Conversational content	Behavioural features	Usefulness
Stage 4: Love	"You're gorgeous," to whoever happens to be in his presence irrespective of gender, sexual orientation, attractiveness or indeed human or not.	Mainly sedentary with occasional horizontal interludes.	Most likely to make ridiculous (but widely witnessed) promises relating to payrises and promotion.
Stage 5: Gutter	Similar to the male lead in a softcore porn movie.	As David Attenborough might say, "and here deep in the heart of the Peckham rain forests, settling down for the night in his natural habitat of excrement and vomit, we find the *magnus bullshitatis*, the Strategic Executive."	Photo opportunity for blackmail.

Humiliating though all this can be, the Strategic Executive, mindful of these dangers, can avoid them by leaving early or not turning up to the party at all, so it's best not to put too much store by this fleeting annual moment. It's a bit like choosing for your honeymoon a "follow the

Wildebeast of Kenya" safari trip the one year they decide to base their route on one recommended by Transport for London's website and take a succession of inefficiently disjointed bus routes.

But do not fear – all is not lost for there is one area where Mother Nature has seen to it that the Strategic Executive cannot avoid close contact with office juniors. This is the ultimate taboo in the business world: what goes on in the loos.

Look away now

Toilets are the one area which is the great leveller of all workers in the corporate hierarchy Although bosses have managed to engineer separate offices, personalised parking spaces and executive canteens, they haven't yet managed to justify separate toilets. So one minute they might be lording it over the hoi polloi with their talk of how they've revolutionised the organisation's competitive advantage via a business transformation aggressively pursuing an upskilling of an upgraded upmarket up their own arse initiative. And the next - there they are dangling out their knobs next to Joe from the print-room.

It is remarkable how this predicament challenges even the most loquacious of conversationists. You suddenly find yourself facing a sterile white wall, where for once even conversation about the weather seems too inane to pursue. Female readers may very well wonder why we men don't avoid this by just going into one of the cubicles but this would be tantamount to admitting that you're failing in your Toilet Mission Statement, namely, "To be seen as a Real Man."

As male readers will know, there is a whole panoply of etiquette and faux pas associated with toilets, none of which is documented in even the most voluminous of induction manuals or staff handbooks. But what a great relief to the usual dross it would be, so why not cut out the next few paragraphs and slip it in at the next available opportunity?

Apart from minor ancillary challenges such as working out how the hell to get the hand-dryer to work and how to open the bin for disposing of the paper towels (assuming you can find it in the first place), the main challenges present themselves at the urinal. The basic goal is to maintain an entirely superficial conversation about a current topical event, whilst the act of urination has to be conducted efficiently and without any collateral damage.

An early hazard to be avoided is the one which crops up if, in the rush to get to work on time, you put your boxer shorts on the wrong way round. Thus, on your first loo visit of the day, in a vain attempt to find the opening, now situated at the rear, you will give the appearance of having lost your willy.

Willy duly located and extracted, the key objective is to start the urinal flow quickly, for it to last a reasonable amount of time and for it to stop cleanly without dribbling or secondary spurts. This achievement can then be marked with the customary and unnecessarily protracted ceremonial shaking of the high-performance willy. Remember that mission statement, "To be seen as a Real Man."

As you can imagine there are a number of pitfalls in all this. For instance, for some biological reason, farts cannot be withheld without interrupting the urinal flow. So if you feel a fart coming on, you have to make a lightning choice between *either* suppressing the fart (complete with distended facial expression) but appearing as an incontinent man with a stop-go flow *or* you can keep the pee in full flow but you'll have to let rip with the fart(s) whilst somehow pretending that they are not happening. A challenge made considerably harder by the fact that loo acoustics seem to have been designed to maximise the noise of anal emissions.

However many more dangerous hazards surround the issue of the direction of the penile emission. Principal amongst these is the stray pubic hair over the penile opening which contrives to re-direct the flow in multi-directions or, more unfortunately, in one direction but not the intended one. It's one thing being able to apologise for spitting food over a work colleague during one of those ghastly stand-up buffet lunches, it's quite another apologising for pissing on them.

But of course the ultimate embarrassment is erectile malfunction. As all men know, erections do not know when they are not wanted. Hence the term "cock up" has come to mean a grotesque error, which prima facie is quite odd because most men are quite happy when their cock's up. There are few less wanted appearances of an erection than in the loo (unless you're George Michael). Once committed at the urinal, there's no turning back, so if you've got a massive hard-on, it'll be there for all to see. If this weren't bad enough, the trajectory of urine from the aroused organ is much more vertical than normal often causing the pee to hit the convex shape of the urinal at such an angle that it bounces back towards the face of the urinator. Even whilst this is happening, it is essential to maintain banal toilet talk, "nice weather we're having... apart from the light drizzle perhaps."

Crapping

A complete faux pas is going into the cubicles. Men who do this to wee immediately fail in the Mission Statement and men who do it to crap are in some sense inferior because crapping in the office is not kosher. This is something of a paradox since, although it is most certainly de rigueur for many men to talk crap all day every day, the actual act of crapping in the office is not the "done thing".

If you are going to resort to a cubicle, it is paramount not to be seen entering or leaving it. If someone is already in the loo, you can go to the urinal for a wee and then take an inordinate amount of time drying your hands until the cubicle is vacated. Once in the cubicle, the first task is to meticulously scrub the toilet seat. Despite there being no scientific evidence whatsoever that you can catch anything from sitting

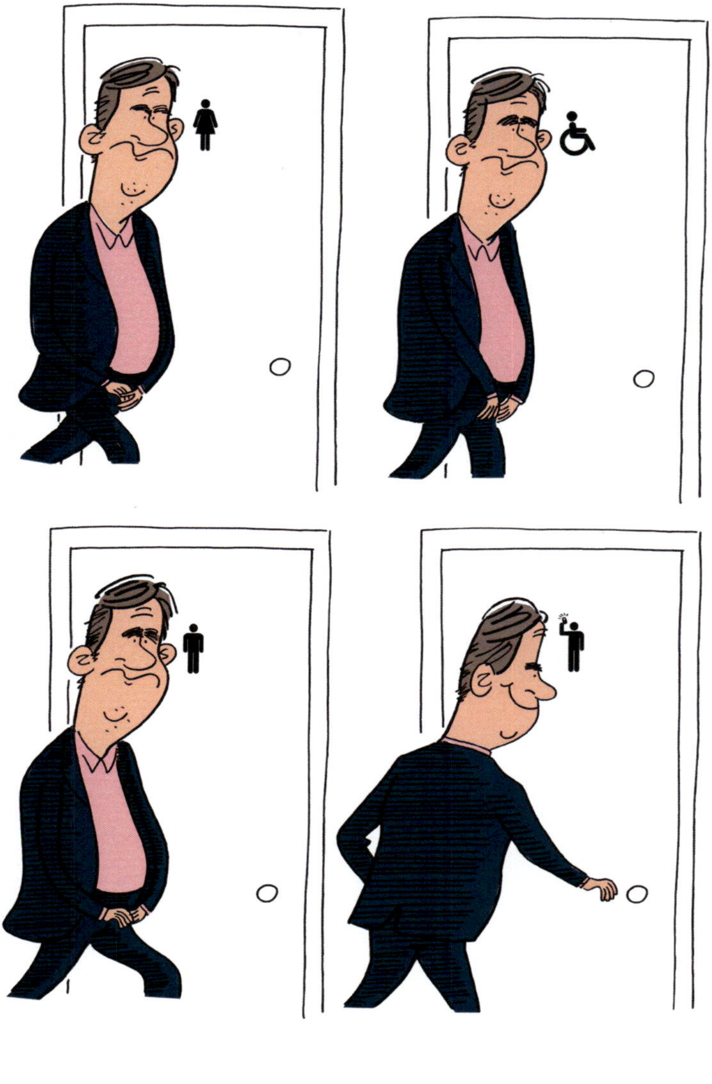

on a toilet seat previously sat upon by anyone else. Cleaning complete and assuming that you've got in the cubicle anonymously and have faith in your exit strategy, it's OK (and in fact quite satisfying) to treat fellow toilet users to a wide and prolonged variety of farting, plopping and grunting noises.

However this is a prelude to the most dangerous part of the whole mission, i.e. making your exit without being noticed. By now the whole toilet will wreak of the smell of your crap. Pulling the chain and exiting immediately is risky since the noise of the flush may mask the sound of someone coming in, so it's much better to just make a run for it whenever you know the coast is clear. This explains why when you arrive in the loo, there's more often than not the deposits of the previous user for all to see.

After that all too brief digression into literal crap, let's go back to the more common forms of crap in the office, namely the behaviours, writings and utterances which we see day in, day out.

XV

TOP 10 RIDICULOUS THINGS ABOUT OFFICE LIFE

In the way that television programme producers are in the habit of throwing together some vaguely linked scraps, getting a few C-list celebrities to make banal remarks about them and then calling it the "Top 100 this, that or the other", this chapter comprises bits and pieces which weren't substantial enough to form a chapter in their own right. Even using advanced Blue Peter link skills, they couldn't somehow be shoe-horned into any other chapter.

The fact that this is a Top 14 and not a round number like 10 is further proof of the left-over nature of the contents of this chapter, so if you haven't enjoyed the earlier parts of this book, it's highly unlikely that you'll get much out of this one.

Anyway, let's countdown those office absurdities.

14   Why do you have to bring cakes to the office on your birthday? Shouldn't it be the other way round?

13   Why is it that, whilst technology is making everything smaller and easier to use, office photocopiers are getting bigger and more and more unfathomable?

12   Token jokes and lame links

Most Strategic Executives have learnt somewhere or other that, if possible, you should start a speech with a joke or some sort of diversion so as to grab the audience's attention. Therefore many have managed to come up with some sort of lame one-liner which vaguely links to the opening section of their tedious drivel.

Something like, "Why did Nick Clegg cross the road? Because he said he wouldn't. This reminds me of when I was crossing the road the other day and I thought, 'our mission statement's great but it could be even greater'." Do we really need these sort of openers? Or should they just be upfront and say, "the next 20 minutes is going to be really dull so I won't raise false hopes by starting off with a half-decent joke"?

11   Suggestions box

When Oliver Twist asked for more, little did he know that he was pioneering the use of office suggestions boxes, i.e. making an entirely reasonable request which would get ignored.

10   Unenforceable office procedures.

Somebody once spent a lot of time writing the constitution for Syria, which, having reminded us that personal freedom is "sacred", goes on to guarantee freedom of assembly, freedom of expression and independence of the judiciary. Similarly divorced from reality are numerous Clean-Desk, IT usage and company mobile 'phone policies. These documents require that employees never use their PCs for private use, never use their mobile 'phones for personal calls and completely tidy their desks at the end of the working day. It's a bit like legislating that men should stop picking their noses.

9   Office drink-ups

Office drink-ups are like being in a lift which gets stuck between two floors. Suddenly you have to make conversation with a random combination of work colleagues. Except that at least in the lift, you don't have to shower gifts on your colleagues. Unlike office drink-ups when someone has to get the first round. Cue the strange ritual of who pays for the drinks. If the boss is there, it's easy: he does. If not, then a sophisticated repertoire of drinks-purchasing avoidance techniques will be on display.

The main feature of these manoeuvring rituals is to ensure that you're not the first to get to the danger zone which is the bar and catch the eye of the waiting barman. So, all of a sudden and entirely out of character, office workers suddenly become desperately chivalrous and open the doors not just for the women, but for fellow work-colleagues or even for passing piss-heads and chavs. Once in the pub everyone suddenly goes into dawdle-and-look-around-the-room mode. Some people make a sudden bolt for the loo or manifest a hitherto unknown interest in wall photographs of local football teams from the 1980s. Those brave enough to order drinks for one or two of their close mates run the horrendous risk that everyone else will just bundle in and add to their round.

The real masters are those who turn up late just after the drinks have been ordered – this has the double advantage of appearing to be working hard and being seen to generously offer everyone a drink, safe in the knowledge that there'll be few takers.

8   Employee satisfaction surveys

Like the FIFA ethics committee, employee satisfaction is a contradiction in terms but nevertheless forms the subject of numerous surveys. It's a bit like asking the leaders of the League Against Cruel Sports what they think of fox-hunting. The results are a foregone conclusion. Likewise staff surveys – people want more money, fewer bosses and better communication. The "action plan" which senior management invariably promises in response to the survey, but never delivers, would, if it were to faithfully follow the desires of the respondents, involve the Strategic Executive team taking a nice boat trip off the Somali coast.

7   Excuses for being sick (snow, stress, volcanic ash, etc). Whereas Alexander the Great *died* from food poisoning, Siobhan on reception regularly survives from this scurge which has a noticeable propensity to strike on Fridays and with no known recorded instances on a Bank Holiday Monday. And isn't it remarkable how many self-centred egotists require "compassionate" leave to attend the funerals of the father of their ex-girlfriend's best friend's flat-mate's next-door

neighbour? If you recognise yourself in this section, then, if only for the sake of originality, why not invent an illness? Or take an existing disease and apply a multiple to it? "Double pneumonia", "Triple migraine", "quadruple hangover". If you're daring, you could name a new condition after a colleague you particularly dislike, e.g. Murdoch Syndrome for dysfunctional somnia. Sounds so much better than, "I couldn't be bothered to get up."

6   Management by walking about. Oh dear.

5   Fire! Fire!

Health & Safety rules require that you ascertain the disabilities of people on your office premises since, for example, if there had to be an evacuation, you'd need to know if anyone had any "special requirements". As if saving your life isn't one. Anyway that's all very reasonable except that one of the so-called "disabilities" is pregnancy. Now how on earth did the people who framed this legislation think that this information was meant to be obtained? Perhaps in future, the

Health & Safety approved English phrase book will record that the recommended way for office receptionists to greet visitors is, "How do you do? Are you pregnant?"

4   Symbolism

Let's face it – offices are boring; they're all the same and we can't wait to get out of them. Then why oh why do Strategic Executives regularly invoke analogies and symbolism, which we then compare to our humdrum monotony.

Popular comparisons are to sporting teams, e.g. to Ryder Cup winners. This is so that the Strategic Executive can massage his own ego by saying that the team comprises brilliant individuals (i.e. himself and, for example, Tiger Woods, before he turned out to be a complete shyster) but also lesser mortals who "work well in the team", i.e. cash in on the talent of the others. Unfortunately Strategic Executives rarely plan in advance so an analogy which is superficially attractive and starts off well can often go seriously wrong. For example…

Strategic Executives likening their company to a Formula 1 racing team is a popular one. Everyone working efficiently on their defined roles, all four tyres of a car can be changed within three seconds so that the vehicle can speed off back into the fast lane in double quick time. What a very apt analogy for business - you end up with something making a load of noise, going round in circles and generally polluting everything around it. And of course it might crash.

Perhaps sporting symbolism is used to rationalise how Strategic Executives spend their time. They would like to think that, just as Francis Drake happened to defeat the Spanish Armada whilst playing a game of bowls, they can spend their Friday afternoons playing golf and still conquer the far eastern markets.

Mind you, you have to give credit for some of the symbolism people manage to make up. For instance there are religious people who believe that the cross is the word "I" crossed out, indicating Jesus's lack of egoism. This is all very well except that Jesus didn't speak English and the word for "I" in Hebrew is "אני" which would have made for a very strange crucifixion.

3   Dress-down Friday

Dress-down Friday is for Strategic Executives a sort of sponsored "Avoidance of Personal Grooming" day. In a failed attempt to look sporty, casual and 15 years younger than they actually are, one day a week, they don't shave, don't comb their hair and don't dress properly. In fact their abandonment of basic personal hygiene on these days is so absolute that when you see a Strategic Executive coming out of the toilet, you can be sure he hasn't washed his hands, so, if you have to shake hands, just pray that he did at least wipe his bottom.

2   Office tours

On various occasions, people are taken on office tours. This has got to be the dullest imaginable way to spend an hour (apart perhaps from "An Evening with Ed Miliband"). "Here is a group of people sitting at their desk......and over here.....we have some more people sitting at their desks. Would you like to come over here and see our relationship management team sitting at their desks? Look there's somebody making a 'phone call. And Johnny here is using the photocopier." Unfortunately the people being taken on the tour (new starters, prospective purchasers, potential suppliers) are all on best behaviour and therefore draw upon all their reserves of politeness to grunt out platitudinous remarks such as, "lovely office, nice carpet, I like the coffee machine." This all feeds the myth that office tours are worthwhile and interesting. When will someone have the guts to say, "this is sooooo boring"?

1   Ultimate Danger

What is the most dangerous thing we do in our lives? Given the statistics about road safety, driving to work? Or crossing the road? Even catching a train or tube? Or what about hazardous weekend pursuits, like abseiling, sky-diving or mountaineering whilst relying on Google Earth as your only map? Not to mention life-threatening habits like smoking and drinking? Nope, none of these. The only thing our dear old friend the Health & Safety Officer considers worthy of a "risk assessment" is our workstation.

Exactly what risk is being assessed? Might the desk suddenly jump up and bite us? Or maybe the chair will mutate into a jet engine's cockpit and spontaneously activate the eject button? And that computer has always looked a bit suspicious, especially with its so-called "mouse" which bears a tell-tale resemblance to a bomb fuse.

If the risk assessment's existence is farcical, then its actual operation is highly comical. The assessor will commence by asking their victim to sit in his or her "normal position". Of course this is quite impossible when you are a) thinking about it and b) being watched by a nurd with a clipboard. The employee therefore adopts a totally false position complete with bolt upright back, curious Mona Lisa smile and hands placed on the desk in the way that Pamela Stephenson used to impersonate Jan Leeming.

There then follow a string of nursery school style questions, such as, "show me how you answer the 'phone," "type an e-mail for me" and "have a dump" (perhaps not). All of which trigger some equally artificial responses – a bit like you might imagine Margaret Thatcher impersonating C3PO from "Star Wars." This bizarre behaviour gives the Risk Assessor plenty to write about and, since they do this all day every day, they must form the view that Britain's offices are staffed by the extended family of Mr Bean.

But the menace of the office environment is not only reflected in the need for risk assessments. People go on courses to train to be certified "First Aiders" and there are of course also trained Fire Wardens who spring to life during the fire drill (the time and date of which everyone knows well in advance, not least because it marks the centenary of the last one).

Perhaps it's a bit unkind to give our Health & Safety friends two entries in the Top 5 Office Absurdities. You may conclude from this that Health & Safety officers are the most ridiculous thing in the office. Not so, because really *the* ultimate ridiculous aspect of office life, the one thing which makes the Strategic Executives look good, when in fact they are rubbish is a word that nobody dares criticise. Technology.

XVI

BOYS AND THEIR TOYS

For the Strategic Executive, "technology" is a magic word which means "always good". The words "Dubai" and "alloy wheels" fall into the same category. Strategic Executives talk about, "embracing technology," almost as much as they do about, "embracing change." All this eulogising of constant change makes you wonder how they feel about long-term relationships and marriage: the bit about, "'til death us do part," must be particularly difficult for them.

"Embracing change" is a mindless mantra which forms an intrinsic part of the Strategic Executive's superficial world-view. Rather like magpies, with whom Strategic Executives share a similar IQ, they can't help but be attracted to sparkly little toys.

If "technology" means "always good", then "spending" means "always bad". The Strategic Executive never spends company money, he always *invests* it. Readers who are financially astute may be surprised at the Strategic Executive's diversified portfolio of investment vehicles for company money which takes in rounds of golf and trips to lap-dancing clubs.

Another bad word is "conservative". Not because it's the name of the political party which is a bit soft on immigration and which keeps overlooking his much-merited OBE but conservatism in the sense of status quo. And not the crap rock group which, like the Strategic Executive, made a career out of repeating the same three things ad nauseam. Conservatism in the sense of resistance to change. And if the Strategic Executive embraces change as he would his wife, then conservatism is his mistress. Publicly he denies any relationship with it, but there are aspects of her which he can't let go, e.g. perks, bonuses and a nice office.

So why is technology such a great thing for Strategic Executives? Most new technologies present people with an excuse not to do a chore. This was quite helpful when, say, the invention of the house stopped people being at the mercy of wolves. It was less helpful when things like calculators stopped people being able to add up. Not long after, the advent of mobile 'phones obviated the need for planning your day. GPS meant you didn't need to plan your route and predictive texting and spellcheck got round the requirement to master English. Little wonder then that business is dominated by people who can't write or add, don't know what day it is or where they're going.

For normal people, however, the most obvious retort to most new technological inventions is, "What's the point of that?" Not so for the Strategic Executive – if he were one of the dragons in Dragon's Den, they'd have to re-name it "Father Christmas's grotto", so freely would he be distributing cash to all and sundry. The "What's the point of that?" question is one that a Strategic Executive will never ask (another one is, "What would you like to drink?"). It suggests a Luddite lack of imagination. Confronted by a vacuum in a void, the Strategic Executive will see value where there is none (like fans of Justin Bieber). In these sorts of situations he can always be relied upon to muster something like, "I can see a number of uses for this but what specifically did you have in mind?"

Of course the apotheosis (or is it the nadir?) of modern technology is the BlackBerry, named after a fruit which is most commonly observed in bird poo. It's a type of "Smart 'phone". Wish you could say the same for its users. The BlackBerry enables the Strategic Executive to get brownie points from his boss for conspicuously dealing with an e-mail at 3 p.m. on a Sunday as opposed to unobtrusively (and more effectively) dealing with it at 10 a.m. on a Monday. The fact that the Sunday action is trite and ineffective is entirely academic; the Strategic Executive has achieved his objective of being seen to be operational "24/7".

Technology has become a fundamental part of the Strategic Executive's life. In fact a diabetic deprived of a dialysis machine will last much longer than a Strategic Executive whose BlackBerry has crashed. At first his fingers will quiver like a heroine addict doing cold turkey, then he starts to rant in a deranged, incomprehensible manner (difficult to differentiate from when he's feeling fine). Mercifully, first aiders are now trained in how to deal with such emergencies. Turn off the BlackBerry, wait patiently for a minute (an alien concept to Strategic Executives) and then re-start. Why oh why doesn't this work with cars?

Of course there are some forms of technology (old and new) which, however advanced they become, will never be "embraced" by the Strategic Executives. Photocopiers, dishwashers and coat hangers for instance. The use of these devices is a matter for automatic delegation. The dishwasher is particularly out of bounds since it is situated in the self-imposed no-go zone which is the kitchen. Which nicely leads us into a "through the keyhole" peep into the Strategic Executive's residence.

Chez l'executive stratégique

In his own home, the Strategic Executive can use technology as he sees

For the modern Strategic Executive,
work-life balance is paramount so…

after a long day in the office,
it's important to find the time……

to work.

fit. His home is not so much nouveau riche as nouveau prétentieux. It will be in a gated, new-build estate, the function of the gates being ambiguous – is it to keep the riff-raff out or the Strategic Executives in?

Strategic Executives have the taste of premier league footballers: everywhere is white or magnolia and very pristine. Their way of making guests feel at home is to tell them to take their shoes off on arrival, so as not to sully the immaculate shag-pile carpet. The design appears to be based upon a Multiplex cinema complex with big screens plastered on the walls in all rooms, popcorn and sweets readily available and enough toilets to cater for dozens of people at a time.

Apart from the kitchen, the main No-go zone for the Strategic Executive is the garden. This is due to its inextricable links with concepts entirely alien to the Strategic Executive, namely fresh air, physical labour and tranquillity. But there is one occasion when the Strategic Executive will venture out there – his annual Bar BQ party. As a manifestation of his averseness to the great outdoors, he will do his damnedest to make the area as in-doors as possible with outdoor heaters, gas-powered BarBQ, floodlights and naff music.

Friends and family and anyone else the Strategic Executive wants to show off to will receive an invitation along the lines of…..

INVITATION
Mr and Mrs Double-Barrelled
Invite
Their equally obnoxious neighbours
To a BarBQ
featuring
Too much food, served up much too late
Dress code: Pseudo-cool
Conversation topics: Expected movements in house prices
4x4s: Midnight

Back to the future

Whilst on the subject of technology, it must be appropriate to end this book in the style of the Strategic Executives – engaging in a pot pourri of wild speculations about the future. Only this time it's the future of the Strategic Executives themselves which will be the subject matter.

Strategic Executives love thinking ahead (as opposed to thinking with their heads). Just like historians on TV programmes come to some outrageous conclusion on the basis of a bit of flint they've found in an abandoned chalk quarry, they engage in flights of fantasy culminating in preposterous hallucinations about the Business World of Tomorrow. This is what they call "blue sky thinking". More like dementia.

Often the technological fantasies they conjure up involve a world where a machine will be invented which automatically does something that they currently are inept at. This gives the appearance that their perceived weaknesses are in fact just a symptom of being ahead of their time. Wouldn't they just love to read, "scientists in silicon valley are already close to developing the auto-chaser which enables Outlook to read a deadline in an e-mail and send out a follow up mail without the sender doing anything."

Another daily challenge they could really do without is tying their shoelaces. This is a particularly hazardous task for the disproportionately large number of Strategic Executives with a roly-poly profile which can mean that this activity incurs the very real risk of toppling over. A 1970s toy advert used to proclaim, "Weebles wobble but they don't fall down." Strategic Executives aren't so fortunate and now I've mentioned this, you'll notice that you never one tying his shoelace. In order to circumvent this daily hazard, the Strategic Executive of Tomorrow will come to work barefoot, no doubt in the process alluding to such barefoot icons as Gandhi, Joss Stone or Fred Flintstone.

A technological innovation that the Strategic Executive is really craving for is the waterproof BlackBerry. This would mean that one of the few public spaces which to date have remained safe havens from Strategic Executives – the swimming pool – would be invaded. Imagine your route up the fast lane being blocked by a man-walrus standing there spouting on about, "a trust-based culture leveraging our channels to market to bring about a step-change in real-time collaboration in….blah blah blah". For God's sake, please someone drown him.

Returning to the Strategic Executives themselves, what will they be like in 50 years' time? Well, dead of course but what about their successors? Some aspects can fairly safely be predicted by simply extrapolating current trends. Take language, for instance.

Je parle le bullshit

Anyone who has read the works of Chaucer will be surprised to learn that it is written in English. Language evolves over time, sometimes out of all recognition. The great innovators of the English language in the twenty-first century are Strategic Executives. They've abolished adverbs, converted nouns into verbs ("to strategise", "to architect") and verbs into nouns ("disconnect"). Only conjunctions and prepositions (words like "if", "but" and "and") – protected by being monosyllabic - have been spared but it can't be long before they are targeted.

Amongst their more inspired linguistic innovations has been adding the words "up" and "out" to the end of the words for no apparent reason. Thus a report is now a "Report-out" and instead of *contacting* someone, you "reach out" to them. Ironically the words ending in "–up" which most readily come to mind when thinking of Strategic Executives, namely cock-up and piss-up, do not feature so frequently in their vocabulary. Some of their lingustic inventions show a frightening ignorance of elementary biology – they will refer to "living documents" and instead of warning you, a Strategic Executive will give you your own personal "heads up" thus suggesting that he seems to be unaware that humans are single-headed.

Furthermore they are developing a range of metaphors showing an ever increasing degree of familiarity. So, "singing from the same hymn sheet," has become, "being on the same page." More disconcertingly expressions such as "customer intimacy" and "market penetration" are readily bandied about. A merger of two companies will be described as, "getting into bed."

Over the centuries the English language has been enriched by foreign invaders – Latin came with the Romans and French with the Normans and now we have Japanese coming with the Strategic Executives. By expressing simple ideas in Japanese, the Strategic Executive's juvenile, knee-jerk remarks take on an apparent intelligence out of all proportion to their underlying quality. Let's hope this doesn't go the same way as Shakespeare where incomprehensible gibberish, interspersed with Medieval profanities, is over-acted and then lauded by the blue rinse brigade who haven't the faintest idea what's going on.

Or, alternatively, if you want to appear very progressive in your use of business-speak, why not make up some of this nonsense yourself and see what happens? It's quite easy – think of what you want to say, convert the noun to a verb, throw in a bit of mock Japanese and then announce to your colleagues that you're going to "tripise Paris-up with a hasha kana." Of course they may think you're off to see a prostitute but who cares, you seem very avant-garde.

The Strategic Executive of Tomorrow

But the most awe-inspiring vision of the future revolves around the very fusion of technology with the Strategic Executive himself. Nowadays

Looking ahead I envision a future where Saftware trans-lates our thoughts instantly into presentations...
Where hunger-recognition robots automatically Serve up 3 Star Michelin meals
and where droid driven cars ferry us from meetings by downloading our calenders...
Amazing... One day we may even have a woman on the board.

the insertion of the letter "I" in front of a word can revitalise a tired concept. Thus i-Phone, i-Pad, i-Pod, i-commerce, etc. It hasn't always worked, IDS, IMF and Isle of Wight, for example. Also there are some rather frightening twists which this trend might take: for instance what would we make of an I-bank, given the complete shambles that the normal ones have created? But this concept still has some considerable mileage left in it. And so, ladies and gentleman, I present the Strategic Executive of Tomorrow, the i-Prat.

The i-Prat is a sort of Pope mobile for the Strategic Executive who is welded inside. Strategic Executive language is pretty formulaic so modern computer geeks are more than capable of programming auto-response lines into the i-Prat. The i-Prat comes in a flatpack with assembly instructions provided by IKEA so it can be readily constructed within the space of just two quick years. Here's a preview of the Instructions for the i-Prat, which have been translated from Samsungese into English.

Instructions for the use of your i-Prat

- To insert batteries: open mouth and stuff a load of chips in twice a day.
- To activate, position besides an attractive female or shout the word "bonus".
- Your i-Prat comes with multi-functionality. You just press one of the following buttons:

Button	Function
Name selector	This authentic feature means your i-Prat can randomly generate names when talking to people just like a real Strategic Executive.
Strategic insight	Press this button for some indecipherable gobbledegook.
Decision	This button does not work properly.
Only available on more advanced models – the i-Git	
Management by walking about	With a fixed grin your i-Git will circulate on predetermined routes, making inane remarks and pretending to recognise people.
Appraisal meeting	Complete with bored nodding and the generation of preposterous objectives.
Troubleshooting tips	Shoot the cause of the trouble, the Strategic Executive.
Decision	Press the button entitled, "Jump to the wrong conclusion".

The future's bright, the future's strategic

And so here we are on the penultimate paragraph. This is also the last paragraph that the Strategic Executive *won't* read since one of the rules of "skim reading" is that you read the introduction and then skip straight to the end. So the paragraph below is just for Strategic Executives: the real conclusion is here. I'm hoping that, on the basis of the following paragraph, Strategic Executives throughout the land will recommend this book to their work colleagues. After all, I don't really want Strategic Executives to die out – I need them to continue so that I can, like business book writers, have a chance of cashing in with a lame sequel. You see, perhaps there's a bit of a Strategic Executive in all of us.

STRATEGIC EXECUTIVE SUMMARY

On reflection I was wrong in the introduction: Strategic Executives are inspirational rocks of talent in an ocean of mediocrity. Having looked at the wondrous phenomena that are banks, business books and HR and having analysed the writing and presentation skills of the modern Strategic Executive, you can't help but be in awe of their all-round vision and almost super-human insight and capabilities. The Strategic Executive is the saviour of the modern world. Long may they continue.